The social history of Canada

MICHAEL BLISS, EDITOR

THE LETTERS OF WILLEM DE GELDER 1910-13

A Dutch homesteader on the prairies

TRANSLATED AND INTRODUCED BY

HERMAN GANZEVOORT

UNIVERSITY OF TORONTO PRESS

© University of Toronto Press 1973

Toronto and Buffalo

Printed in Canada

ISBN (clothbound) 0-8020-2071-2

ISBN (paperbound) 0-8020-6192-3

LC 73-85658

An introduction

BY HERMAN GANZEVOORT

FEW HOMESTEADERS in the Canadian west had the time, interest, or education to reflect upon and record the incidents of their daily life. Most first-hand accounts of the opening and settlement of the prairies are reminiscences written long after the events. Coloured by the passage of time, they tend to highlight the significant or memorable occurrences in the homesteader's life, while glossing over the day-to-day details and drudgery of the settler's hard fight to survive and succeed in a new life. The letters in this volume, found in the original Dutch in the Archives of the Netherlands Emigration Service in Holland, form a unique chronicle of the life of one European homesteader in Saskatchewan from 1910 to 1913. Their author's experience as a homesteader was typical of that of hundreds of thousands of newcomers to the prairies in the greatest years of western expansion just before World War I. As a European immigrant in Canada, however, he writes from a special perspective often ignored in Anglo-Saxon accounts of western development.

These letters were written to someone in Holland whose identity remains unknown. The only reference to the sender's name is an enigmatic Bill or Will. I began translating the letters in the summer of 1971 as part of a larger study of Dutch immigration to Canada and became more and more interested in the identity and history of the man who had written so minutely and perceptively about his daily life. Knowing he had homesteaded in Log Valley, Saskatchewan, twenty miles north of Morse, I placed an advertisement in the nearest newspaper, *The Swift Current Sun*. Almost 58 years after the last letter had been written, his friends and acquaintances and those who had heard of him from family and neighbours wrote to tell me what they knew or remembered. Their recollections enabled me to piece together a portrait of a singular man.

Willem or Bill De Gelder was born in the 1880s in Doorn in the Netherlands. He was the son of a well-to-do banker and received all the benefits of birth in an upper-class home. He attended and graduated from the University of Leyden at a time when a university education was a privilege reserved to a select few. De Gelder apparently travelled extensively on the continent and was fluent in seven languages, including classical Greek. We might assume that he was a restless young man searching for experiences beyond the borders of his small homeland; it must have been this spirit which sent him to

Canada in the spring of 1910, perhaps as a result of a public lecture
on Canada which he mentions attending.

Canada was a popular topic of discussion in Holland during these
years, for like the Scandinavian countries, Holland was considered
prime recruiting ground by Canadian agents interested in attracting
the most 'racially' fit immigrants to Canada. The ordinary Hollander
could not speak English, but he was apt to be clean, hard-working,
Protestant, and of Nordic stock. Several Dutch-Canadians toured the
Netherlands on behalf of Canadian companies presenting magic
lantern shows and lectures depicting the good life to be had in
Canada. The priest mentioned in De Gelder's letters was almost
certainly Father Van Aken of Helena, Montana, who toured the
Netherlands on behalf of the Canadian Pacific Railway to recruit
settlers for the irrigated farms at Strathmore, Alberta, recruiting 98
families in 1908 and 1909.

Van Aken received his commission, but the settlers lost their
stake and drifted off the land, giving rise to De Gelder's bitter
comments and confirming the Dutch government's feeling (in con-
trast to some other European governments) that it had little to
worry about from Canadian immigration agents. For the most part,
the Dutch populace was not particularly interested in starting a new
life in a strange land. Those who were overpowered by wanderlust
could always go to Surinam or the Dutch East Indies. The hazards of
settlement in Canada – the bitter climate, untamed territory, and
venal land sharks – were all too well described in Dutch newspapers
and magazines. If America did become an irresistible dream, the
prospering Dutch settlements in Michigan, Iowa, and Washington
offered a chance to settle among one's own countrymen.

Yet, there were always exceptions to the rule and a trickle of
Dutch immigrants did flow to the Canadian west. Many of the
immigrants settled in predominantly urban areas, unwilling to under-
go the hardships of homesteading. Many were adventurous young
men, drifting from one job to another, from one place to another,
and often either returning to the Netherlands or moving on to the
United States or South America. A few experiments in community
settlement were tried in Neerlandia, Granum, and Monarch, Alberta,
and in Edam, Saskatchewan, but despite some initial success they
never fulfilled the dreams of their founders. Still, there were those
such as De Gelder who did establish their stake in the new society,

overcoming drought, prairie fire, loneliness, and all the other hazards of homesteading. Their fortitude and endurance explained the reputation Hollanders established as being among the best settlers obtainable for the prairies, a feeling about Dutch immigrants which has been maintained, in varying degrees, until the present.

Unlike many of his fellows, De Gelder had the monetary resources to leave Holland once he had succumbed to the emigration fever. Nevertheless, it seems that he travelled under the aegis of the Salvation Army on one of their immigrant charter ships. In the first decade of this century the Salvation Army became quite active in the recruitment and placement of immigrants. The bulk of the traffic came from the United Kingdom, but continental emigrants were encouraged to use the Army's services, too. The Toronto Salvation Army Citadel actively advertised across Canada for jobs in all areas of employment. Requests were categorized, and on shipboard an attempt was made to match jobs and immigrants. Although this service was not obligatory, the majority of those who travelled, having little information about Canada, accepted it willingly. De Gelder seems to have been one of these. Some immigrants were assisted with passage money on the agreement that the employers would reimburse the Army from the immigrants' wages.

De Gelder travelled by steerage and bought his ticket to Winnipeg in Holland. He complains of the treatment meted out by the immigration officals to steerage passengers and comments on the extra expense of Canadian train tickets purchased in Holland. His various warnings to prospective emigrants, amounting to injunctions to trust no one and believe nothing, remind us that Canada initially appeared to the immigrant as a society of confidence men, land sharks, and cheats. He also warns against the Salvation Army, which first placed him on the farm of 'E.' and found him his second job with a Mr Burrill in Elgin, Manitoba. Perhaps De Gelder was soured by the hard life he endured on these farms, or perhaps the good intentions and idealism which gave the Salvation Army its high reputation were no protection against the self-interested cynicism of those with whom the immigrants had to deal.

Like most of his fellow immigrants, De Gelder came to Canada as a hired hand. This working experience was to give him a period of time in which to learn Canadian farming methods, accustom himself to Canadian society, and accumulate capital to start on his own.

Like countless others, he came to realize that many western farmers
were only interested in accumulating their own capital and that farm
labour meant carrying out the jobs no one else wanted, long hours of
back-breaking work, uncertain wages, and usually unemployment in
winter. Because of his poor crop, Burrill was unable to pay De
Gelder his full wage, forcing him to undertake a series of jobs on a
threshing gang, railroad gangs, and finally as a janitor. In this bleak
winter during which he barely survived (once going four days without eating while between jobs), De Gelder's morale seems to have
reached a low point. His dismay at the habits of his fellow bunk-
housemen reinforced his isolation and reflected a not uncommon
reaction of westerners to lower-class foreigners and slum-bred Englishmen. With his own commitment to frugality, sobriety, and
honest work, the Dutchman, De Gelder, was closer to the dominant
values of western society than were many other immigrants.

On 18 July 1911, he filed for his homestead, 20 miles north of
Morse, Saskatchewan. He received his patent for it on 10 October
1914 and the patent for the adjoining south-west quarter section on
11 October 1921. The bulk of his letters are a description of the first
thirty months of his homesteading, beginning with the first winter
on his land, describing his life in fascinating detail, and ending with
his regret at not having accomplished more, largely because he chose
to break land with horses rather than oxen.

De Gelder's letters are a rich source of both the trivial and the
significant in a homesteader's life. He teaches us about the construction of sod huts and tarpaper shacks, thawing frozen eggs and baking
bread, digging wells, keeping feet healthy, and the efficiency of
oxen. Above all, he instructs us in the personal economies of every
aspect of homesteading, varying from his discovery of the merits of
'shopping at Eaton's' to his exhaustive financial accounting in the
autumn of 1913. De Gelder reminds us of the mobility and versa-
tility of the homesteader, of the co-operation (though often bought
and paid for) that characterized the establishment of a successful
farm, and of the narrowness of the settler's margin of success:
'Surely a person has a chance to get ahead here, as he has nowhere
else, but in order to get that chance, he has to say good-bye to an
awful lot' (7 December 1911).

And yet, the nagging question remains: Who was Bill De Gelder?
This series of letters, reproduced from the originals without

abbreviation, is obviously truncated and inconclusive. References to family and friends seem to be missing and the correspondence often becomes a diarist's recall of daily events. I suspect that this series of letters was directed to family members in Holland and that personal references were excised when the surviving copies were made for the use of a Dutch emigration society. The society then used the letters as source material for their own information and in the preparation of literature for other emigrants. This would account for the lack of last names and the personal feeling and emotion which one would expect to fill the letters. The De Gelder who emerges from these letters – cold and often self-centred – bears little relation to the man who is fondly remembered by his friends and neighbours. They describe him as well-built, medium-sized man of good humour. One correspondent, at the time a very young child, remembers him bringing her a khaki soldier doll; another can still picture the day he presented her family with a pail of jam. All agree he was well liked, an interesting visitor, and a good story teller.

De Gelder, however, had few intimate friends. Those who gained his confidence remark on his secretiveness, yet they accepted it and speak with great hesitation because they feel compelled to preserve the cloak of privacy which De Gelder placed around his personal life. He spoke little of his background or his family and only occasionally did a fact or reminiscence give some insight into his past. He was a fine scholar, capable of reading the Greek sermon notes of a visiting Anglican divine or engaging in deep philosophical or theological discussions. He was an avid reader and amateur astronomer, and his most prized possessions were his sky map and the books which lay piled on a desk under his shack's only window. During a violent hail storm, which destroyed this window, De Gelder was observed placing his posterior in the empty frame to protect his books. He commented that he had nothing else as convenient or impervious. He had a puckish sense of humour, which often resulted in practical jokes and some discomfort to his neighbours. As he was the only person in Log Valley with a camera, he assumed the role of neighbourhood photographer and chronicled the events of homestead life. Asked by a neighbour to photograph her in her first fur coat, so that she might send a snap to distant relatives, he quickly complied. The result was a beautiful picture of the coat with the lady's head neatly lopped off. When cameras became common in the area, De Gelder made certain never to be photographed and not one picture of him survives. His friends respected his attempt at maintaining his anonymity, for it was a western tradition never to enquire too closely about another's past lest one's own be opened for public scrutiny.

Even with De Gelder's intimate friends, a certain distance remained in the relationship. He had a healthy and virile interest in women, and like many of his contemporaries he made regular visits to Moose Jaw or Regina, but he would never have thought of interfering in the blooming romance of a friend. When marriage became a reality for his best friend, De Gelder disengaged himself and withdrew, unwilling to interfere in any way. This distance from his friends, the separation from his family, and the loneliness and despression of his solitary life on the prairie manifested itself in an annual week-long alcoholic reassessment. Having invited a friend in to watch over him, he would alternate periods of drinking and staring out the window with an almost comatose sleep. However, he never became violent and when the week was over he would return to his tasks, his period of examination having ended.

De Gelder was better educated than most of his neighbours, but was never accused of any intellectual aloofness or pride. He had sources of capital not shared by the ordinary homesteader and although he worked extraordinarily diligently at his accounts, there is evidence that his family subsidized him in his later homesteading efforts with annual remittances of up to $1000. In later years, De Gelder returned this money when he realized that some of his fellow homesteaders were not only living on what they made, but were sending money home to relatives who were in poor circumstances. The family also sent over Janus Besteboer, a clerk in the family bank, to look after De Gelder and to help him with his homesteading. Besteboer was in essence his watchdog and helpmate, and one can feel at times the friction that developed between them. Besteboer had served in the Dutch East Indies Army before entering the De Gelder bank and as a pensioned sergeant in that service he also had alternate sources of income. While De Gelder's personal hygiene at times left things to be desired, Besteboer thought nothing of rolling up in an old tarpaulin completely dressed and sleeping under the bulging, dripping walls of his sod shack. Needless to say, his army experiences had inured him to discomfort and they stood him in good stead in the Canadian west.

Unlike most North Americans on the Canadian prairies in these years, De Gelder and Besteboer were unfamiliar with the techniques of western farming. Nevertheless, De Gelder seems to have farmed as well as his neighbours. The letters show that he was a hard and persistent worker who learned quickly and well. He made great use of the technical facilities of the agricultural universities both in Canada and abroad. He continually sent samples of soils and grasses for evaluation and guided his farming practices accordingly. The location of his homestead gave him a certain advantage over other western farmers, for his area could support either wheat farming or ranching, although as these letters end, De Gelder regrets having gone into wheat instead of cattle.

As an unmarried man, De Gelder was typical of many of his immediate neighbours and of a majority of the new settlers on the prairies. He would perhaps have been more prone to loneliness without Besteboer, but he was free from many of the tribulations of the married homesteader. He mentions the fact that he must pay school taxes, but only as an aside, and he had no part in establishing the school or worrying about the education of children. For his married neighbours, these were real areas of concern. Though not a regular church attender or participant, De Gelder did contribute to the support of the local church. His light-hearted remarks on bachelor cooking and baking and household chores emphasize his single status. Because he is unmarried, he is free to leave his homestead and work on threshing gangs or go into town frequently. Bachelorhood left him options which married settlers did not have or exercised only in dire emergencies. A family with small children could be a terrible hardship to a homesteader, especially when winter work in lumber camps or the city meant survival.

De Gelder has little to say about the specific problems of being a foreigner in Canadian society. The reasons for this, however, are clear from his letters. He not only knew English before he arrived, but deliberately tried to become Canadian in speech and habits. Asked why he did not settle with other Hollanders, he is known to have commented that if that had been his wish, he would have stayed in Holland. For, 'as soon as you land,' he advises, 'lay aside

your differences ... talk English with everyone, even amongst yourselves, forget your Dutch. Introduce yourself to everyone and talk
with them, but don't believe anything about Canada until you have
seen it with your own eyes' (8 March 1912). This willingness to be
assimilated, along with his clear commitment to the values of work
and thrift so highly prized in the Canadian west, explain why De
Gelder and other immigrants like him, Dutch or any other national-
ity, would not be the subjects of Ralph Connor's nativist fears or the
nationalist social gospel of J.S. Woodsworth. De Gelder fit perfectly
the stereotype of the hard-working, upright, intelligent Dutchman or
Scandinavian as opposed to that of the shiftless, ignorant Gallician
or Ukrainian.

The early 1920s marked a watershed in De Gelder's life. He had
become a successful homesteader; he owned a half-section of land,
met his bills, and was an integral part of his community. However, it
seems that in 1922 he rented his land and made another trip to the
Netherlands to see his family. Janus Besteboer had returned to the
Netherlands in 1914; there he married and managed a Ford tractor
agency until his death. In the fall of 1923, De Gelder returned to
Log Valley for a final visit with his friends and to dispose of his
property. Asked where he was planning to go, he only replied that
he had been learning his eighth language – Spanish. He remarked
that being home in the Netherlands made him feel 'like a stray deer
on Broadway,' and so in general terms denied the possibility of any
return home. It was not until his family wrote and asked about his
whereabouts that his neighbours realized that Bill De Gelder had
simply disappeared. Only Andrew Graham, a former partner of his,
understood the reason: 'The reason of his disappearance was a
normal thing. I believe he thought he was responsible for a mental
illness of his mother. His people tried to trace him; but he made a
complete breakaway. Yes, he must be over ninety ... if he's alive.
But, alive or dead, he was a man worth knowing.' Bill De Gelder was
indeed a man worth knowing, as were the others who shared the
homestead adventure. He and his fellows personify the toughness
and persistence of the western pioneer. The family traumas, the
guilt, and the personal fears which culminated in his disappearance
highlight the anguish that all emigrants, new and old, suffer when
they take that almost irrevocable step to begin a new life, that very
step which leads to a new Canadian identity.

ACKNOWLEDGEMENTS

The preparation of this material for publication has involved many people without whose help it would never have been accomplished. Initially, the Canada Council supplied a grant to do research in Dutch immigration. In Holland, the Netherlands Emigration Service graciously provided access to their records and materials and assisted me in the search of their archives. Particular thanks must be extended to Miss Ann Corthals for her untiring work and the Chief Archivist, Heer Muller, for his assistance and co-operation in this task.

My task as translator was greatly eased by many of my fellow immigrants and family who were familiar with archaic and idiomatic Dutch expressions. Mr Andrew Graham of Central Butte, Saskatchewan, Mrs Beatrice Pass of Morse, Saskatchewan, and many other correspondents gave flesh and substance to the central character of this translation, and in so doing helped clear up some of the mystery. Professors R. Craig Brown and Michael Bliss provided the encouragement and assistance to make publication a reality. Mr Allan R. Turner, Provincial Archivist of the Saskatchewan Archives Board, kindly provided the information on land ownership and helped establish the dates of Willem De Gelder's residency in Log Valley.

While this translation is, in a sense, dedicated to the stubborn strength of the western homesteader, I feel it must also be dedicated to my wife, Suzanne, who in great measure shares those virtues of patience, persistence, and good humour, and without whose help none of this would have been possible.

A Dutch homesteader on the prairies

THE LETTERS OF WILLEM DE GELDER 1910-13

ELGIN, 10 JUNE 1910

There is a long interval between my letter from Winnipeg and this one, in fact so great that I have to rack my brains in order to remember all that has happened to me in the intervening time. Why did I wait so long in writing? I wanted to get settled first, and gather impressions, and not write you a subjective report of one day. I've also put a very trying period behind me and I didn't want to write you during this time. There was no use in burdening you with my woes, or one or two days' impressions. But now I'll give you an account of the ups and downs of my life since my last letter.

After I stepped out of the train in Elgin at 5:37 in the afternoon, I telephoned Mr Burrill (it probably sounds strange to you, a telephone on the prairies, but more about that later). I told him that I had received his address from the Salvation Army and asked him if he could use me, and he said he would come and get me at nine that evening. He came in his buggy (a light conveyance, with thin tires, you see them once in a while in Holland where they are called 'Americans'). He's twenty-nine and a Canadian, his grandfather immigrated from England. His farm is about five miles from Elgin (8 km), and on the way we got acquainted. He told me about his *farm* and his family, he's an obliging fellow but unbelievably dumb, like they all are here. He rents his farm and the rent is composed of one-third of the proceeds of the harvest. He has a half section, 320 acres, more than 100 Hectares, 145 *acres wheat,* 35 *acres oats,* and some acres of kitchen garden, potatoes and flax, and the rest pasture. He's married, has a friendly wife and four children, two girls six and eight, a boy of three and a little girl of two.

We're in the middle of the prairies, all flat land, not a single tree, so you can see for miles. In the distance you can see the 'Mountain,' a great pack of bush about forty miles from here, approximately the distance from Utrecht to Arnhem. The 'Mountain' is the border between Canada and the United States. The 'Mountain' is too far away to get wood from. Because there are absolutely no trees, wood is terribly expensive, so you can understand why there are so few buildings here. We have a small house, a kitchen, and bedroom downstairs where the family sleeps. Upstairs is an attic with my bed, a big double bed with sack of hay, a coverlet, and two blankets. There's also a stable for seven horses. The remaining stock is

composed of a sow, a young pig, about forty chickens, more than
one hundred chicks, three cows, two of which are milked, two calves
which always stay in the stable, and three heifers in the pasture.
Also a dog called Topsy, and a cat which has a cute black kitten.
That's the sum and total of the stock.

The work is hard. In the beginning it was almost impossible for
me to do everything the boss ordered. With almost supernatural
exertion I stuck it out, and from day to day the work load got a
little lighter. Up in the morning at 4:30 or 5:00, we work right
through until 9:30 or 10:00 in the evening, sometimes even longer.
This is no small thing for someone who isn't used to such hard work.
Now I'll describe some of the jobs I do. First I have to get the cows
and horses from the pasture and bring them into the stable, but I've
already filled the trough so that they can drink before they go in.
After they're all in and tied up, I give the cows their chop, 2 litres
of a mixture of barley and oats, milled somewhat like rolled oats.
The horses get oats and chop, except for one which is 20 years old,
and he always gets chop, probably because he can't chew the oats.
The other three work horses get oats, while the colts, one is 3, one 2,
and one is a year old, get chop. Then I curry the horses, this is done
in Canada twice a day, and it's a bothersome job because the old
crocks are wild and rambunctious. Around six, while I'm busy, the
boss slowly turns up to do the milking. It takes him about a half an
hour, and when he's finished he takes his pails to the house and puts
the milk in the separator. This is a machine with which you separate
the cream from the milk by centrifuging it. Then he cleans the separator and fries or boils a couple of eggs. That done, around seven, he
calls 'Will' (that's me) for breakfast. Meanwhile I've curried the
horses and cleaned the stall. I'm generally ravenous, and embarrass
myself sometimes with my enormous hunger. Sometimes I get three
boiled eggs, a couple of fried ones, and a piece of meat, mostly pork.
While the boss and I have breakfast, his wife and kids are still asleep.

After breakfast, which is always quickly finished (15 or 20
minutes), back to work. The boss usually tells me at breakfast what
has to be done that day. If he has to take the horses and plow or
harrow, I have to harness them. I bring them to the house, and he
takes them and goes out to the field. He gives me work to do for the
whole morning: pulling out cowslip, there is a lot in the field and
they are very afraid of it, because it chokes the oats and the wheat.

There are inspectors who check to see if the farmer has pulled up the
cowslip, if they aren't satisfied they will give him a few days to get
the job done. If they come back in a few days and the job isn't to
their liking, they send a fellow who takes the stuff out for *big
money.* Another job is to go and poison the gophers, again. You
have to understand that there are thousands of gophers in this country. They are as big as rats, light brown and cause a lot of damage to
the wheat roots. I spend an entire morning with a pail of poison
leaving a spoonful at every hole. They aren't hard jobs, but it isn't
the greatest thing to be under a blazing sun from seven to twelve
without a particle of shade.

And it can be unbelievably hot here, even in the early morning,
sometimes 100 to 110 degrees, and several days ago 115 degrees in
the shade. You probably ask what shade? In the shade of our house.
Sometimes, I have to take oats from one granary to the other or to
the stall, and that's heavy work. And you sweat as if you were in a
steamroom in the bathhouse in Rotterdam. Another time you have
to fence off the pasture. Because there's no wood you have to use
barbed wire. You have to put the posts in at certain measured dis-
tances, first sharpen them with an axe, then dig a hole in the ground
and drive them in with a sledgehammer. To water the animals we
have a pump on an 85-foot-deep well. Then I have to help build a
bridge, not over water, because that we don't have. The bridge is
built between two hills so that a road can be made. Another time I
will get some clay with the horse and wagon, about 15 minutes from
here, and use it as a cement for making a floor in the stable or the
henhouse. When it's twelve o'clock I go in to the stall and give the
calves water and hay, and the horses water and hay and grain. When
they need it, they are let out for a whole day in the pasture.

Then dinner, the woman of the house has fried up some pork and
boiled some potatoes, and they taste better than any banquet. Practically after every meal you have fruit, naturally not fresh, but a
compote of prunes or peaches. At the table there is usually tea at
noon and at supper, sometimes water, always water for breakfast.
The tea is very good here. After dinner, back to work till about
seven, then supper. Supper is finished and then to cleaning the
horses, watering them, and feeding the calves. Before supper I get the
cows out of the field — I put them there after chores in the morning — and feed them. The boss milks them again after supper. After

the horses have had their water, grain, and hay, they are generally left in the pasture for the night. When the work is finished it is nine o'clock, and the sun is slowly going down. Then the plants in the garden are watered, four pails on the rhubarb, four on the tomatoes, one on the wormwood, one on the cabbage, and one on the cucumbers. Then I saw some wood, and chop some kindling to start the stove the next day and keep it burning for cooking. And then Will is ready, 'that is all' the boss says then, and I rest for a half hour or fifteen minutes and admire the lovely sky at sunset.

In the beginning my legs bothered me, especially my feet, they really hurt. Every evening I take a pail of water upstairs and soak my feet and wash my legs, and that helps. It's solitary here. In the beginning it really bothered me to do my work all alone. The boss is mostly on the land or in the house, and as I'm the only hired hand I have to do everything alone. The loneliness has caught up to me several times but it's better now.

The boss is a small-time farmer, what you would call a crofter in Holland. And he knows darn well that he has a hired hand, and he's proud that he can afford one now. I'm his first permanent hired hand, he had a Scotsman before me, but he couldn't stand up to the hard work.

All the land here is occupied and has a sale value of 30 dollars per acre, so no homesteads here. Homesteads are still open in northern Manitoba, Alberta, and Saskatchewan, lands 60 to 80 miles from the railway line, and some hundreds of kilometres. A railway line first gives the land value here because it enables you to transport your products. So there is not much future in that kind of land. Maybe in ten years or so a railway line will be put in, but that is a matter of speculation. And in order to buy or rent a farm you need a lot of capital. Everything is expensive here. A work horse costs 300 dollars, a cow 40, and a chicken a dollar. The situation is entirely different from the one I read about in Holland, and was described by Mr — . Those were certainly the good old days. I made an agreement with the boss that he should first see what I'm worth and then pay me. I hope he will keep me through the winter. It would be nice if I had a place to stay this winter, otherwise I'll have to go to the city, to Winnipeg, and look for work in a factory.

The land is cropped three years in a row, 2 years wheat and one year oats, the fourth year it is uncultivated, that's called 'summer fallow.' Two weeks ago the boss plowed 55 acres which had lain fallow this year, and he harrowed it this week. He's finished now and won't be in the fields until the harvest at the end of September. The end of July means haying and that's awful hot work. I've made acquaintance with it several times, as I had to bring feed hay to the stall. After you have worked a whole day in that glowing hot hay, under the broiling sun, all alone, let me tell you, you lose quite a few drops of sweat. 'Pails full,' Uncle Louis would say. In the evening you're dead tired, innumerable blisters on your hands, and your back feels broken from the continuous bending. Thanks to the water cure I told you about, I wake in the morning a lot less tired. You have to get accustomed to all sorts of things, and I manage to keep my spirits up through everything. It's often sink or swim, but you *must* accustom yourself.

The nearest farmer lives 1½ miles from here, and on the horizon one sees farm houses and granaries. The boss has three granaries in which he keeps his harvest of oats and wheat. The price of wheat is quite susceptible to fluctuation; it varies from 25 cents to $1.25 per bushel (bu.=60 English pounds). When the wheat price is high, the farmer takes his wheat to the elevators (there are 5 in Elgin) and sells it there. He doesn't sell the oats but keeps it in the granary, as he grows it for the horses. Generally an acre produces 20 bushels, but this year is very bad because much has been burned by the sun. If we get some rain yet, then we can hope for 5 bushels per acre, and that will just cover costs, so my hard-earned pennies will probably also be sent down the drain, because they usually pay your salary after the harvest. The boss has debts to pay, because he, like all farmers, buys a lot on time in the city and pays everything after harvest. Even the farm machinery isn't a cash buy, it's also bought on the installment plan, and the boss has some beautiful machinery. For example, he has a wheat cutter which cuts the grain and binds it in sheaves. You hitch your horses to the machine, get up on it, and ride through the field; the sheaves come out the back tied and all. It must be a wonderful sight to see such a machine at work, and it saves a lot of wages, but it isn't cheap at $165.

I wear a flannel undershirt with a shirt over it, that's comfortable, but unfortunately the shirt is white, I mean light, because it gets dirty so easily. Most of the fellows wear dark workshirts, sometimes completely black, and no underpants or undershirts. Everybody is bothered by the blazing sun, blisters on hands — one day I had 22 — sunburn, and so forth. Another plague is the mosquitoes and other insects. There's a Hollander who lives 1½ miles from here on a...

ELGIN, 28 AUGUST 1910

It's strange, but if the truth be told, I don't know the people a hair better than when I first came here. For that matter there's no time to make closer friendships or have a pleasant chat. The boss isn't as friendly as he formerly was. The whole family is oppressed by the bad harvest and the boss is often out of humour and dissatisfied. The bad harvest also has an effect on my pocketbook, the boss told me he couldn't give me more than $10 per month and couldn't keep me this winter. That was quite a disappointment for me because I had figured on $15. But maybe it isn't that bad if I can't stay here this winter, because if I stayed I couldn't earn much, perhaps not a cent. But if I work in a factory I will be able to earn the whole winter through. The boss is dumb and he will stay that way; every day I see that he is dumber than I thought the day before. He lives in his own little world and knows nothing about what goes on outside it. The children don't go to school, as it is the custom in this neighbourhood not to send the children to school until they are 10 or 12 years old. They then stay in town the whole week and come home on Saturday and Sunday, and naturally they don't get any instruction now from pa or ma; 'No Sir, too busy.'

Elgin is a small town with 500 inhabitants, about as big as Linschoten, and it has *five* churches, an Anglican church, one Mennonite church, and three others. All have ministers with good incomes of a $1000 or more dollars, the highest is probably $1500 or $2000. I don't know if the people go to church very often, but the boss went once when a new preacher came, mostly out of curiosity I think. When he came home he said he was a nice fellow and that he would probably get a good salary. Before meals the boss pinches his eyes shut and mumbles a short and unintelligible grace. The children cover their mouths with their hands, and after the grace, shout triumphantly that they have listened.

There's a hotel with a bar and supposedly quite a bit of drinking is done, mostly whiskey but also beer and 'Holland Gin.' In the winter, when there is nothing to do on the farm, the farmers and cowboys are in town all day long, and a lot of drinking is supposed to go on. The five preachers are busy trying to turn Elgin into a dry town, but it doesn't particularly meet with the approval of the citizenry, and for rather strange reasons. They are not opposed to it because it would curtail their drinking, but because the hotelkeeper would lose his livelihood. They can't understand why the preachers are so hostile to him when he is so 'awfully good' to them. Every year he gives them each $50 in the collection plate. He also pays good wages to his help, the two bartenders each get $30 a month, and the two girls each get $20. Real American! The barkeeper makes tremendous money, and he is quite open and above board, and says that he made so much on such and such a day. For example, they had a plowing match in Elgin one day and he took in $1500 over the bar.

They still haven't got a domestic help on the farm, they have been trying to get one, but there are none to be had even for $15 per month; it's enough to make a Dutch domestic's mouth water. The girls prefer the towns and cities where they can also earn good money.

Dinner is composed of a slice of pork sometimes boiled and sometimes fried, and some potatoes (boiled or fried), and bread and butter. Dessert is a dish of compote, mostly prunes, 3 to 7 in number, and everything is topped off with a cup of tea. Sometimes there are vegetables, but it's a real occasion if there are carrots or wax beans, they simply don't care for them. But even a dinner like that tastes marvelous when you've worked hard and only had a frugal breakfast in the morning. The potatoes which they grow here are generally much larger than in Holland, a potato as big as your fist is no curiosity. Disease is uncommon here because the ground is too dry, but potato bugs (a sort of caterpillar) are a scourge. If you don't watch out, they will eat all the leaves off the plant before you know it.

We've been very busy this week and the boss has been going at full speed. The work kept us occupied all last week and the first half of this one. The first couple of days the work really bothered me because the sharp wheat cut my hands and wrists and made small wounds. This was extremely painful, especially in the evenings after work, when the horses were rubbed down and the salty dust irritated my wounds. So I used my imagination; when I went to the field I put on a coat and gloves. That worked fine, however in two days I had mittens, because the fingers were totally worn off, but my fingers had slowly got used to the work anyway. You can see that you can get accustomed to anything.

Stooking the sheaves is pretty hard work, that is it gets heavy when you have to do it the whole day long, in a bare field under a blazing sun. When the grain is ripe you naturally have to cut it as quickly as possible, and every day saved means more bushels for harvesting. And because the boss doesn't want to increase the days it takes to harvest, he increases the length of the day; we begin an hour or an hour and a half earlier and finish two hours later. Just imagine it, up before dawn and finished after sunset. You have to make sure that the stooks are stacked firmly and can withstand a push, in this case a wind, because it can really blow here. Especially on warm days you get a calm, and then a cyclone comes along and upsets everything if it is not set firmly on its feet. Wednesday, this work was finished and we began bringing the sheaves in. The boss and I get the sheaves with a big wagon, and bring them to the yard, where we make big stacks. It's not easy to handle the sheaves with a fork, and lay them just so on the wagon, so that the kernels are towards the inside. This work will probably take two weeks, then a couple of days of threshing and my work will be done here.

The threshing is done mechanically. The boss doesn't own a thresher (one costs $3000). Someone in Elgin has one, and he comes to the farms and threshes for so much a bushel, depending on how easy the grain is to thresh. A machine like that can thresh about 500 to 2500 bushels per day. You begin threshing in the morning at 4:00 o'clock and finish about nine in the evening. All the ordinary chores of the morning have to be done before four, such as currying the horses, feeding, watering, and breakfast for ourselves. Those promise to be hard days, but never mind, they are only a few of these and after the threshing I will get a few days rest. I wrote a letter to the Salvation Army, asking them if they would write me and let me know if they had work for me here or there at about mid-September. I still haven't received an answer. Some days we skip dinner and only have breakfast and supper.

VIRDEN, 20 OCTOBER 1910

As I hastily wrote you on my postcard from Scarth, I went to
Virden (a town a little bigger than Linschoten, 50 miles west of
Elgin) on the advice of a friend. And good advice it was too because
immediately after my arrival and registration at the Alexandra Hotel
I was offered a job on a threshing machine at $2.25 per day. I went
to the job with two other fellows, left my suitcases behind at the
hotel, and took along my travelling rug, my winter coat, and an
extra pair of shoes.
The farmer lived 10 miles from here. We arrived around supper,
and were immediately invited to help ourselves and sit down at a
great big table with all the rest of the harvest hands. I was hired as a
pitcher with one of the other fellows, and the other was hired as a
teamster. Now I'll tell you how things operate in a 'threshgang,' then
you'll be better able to understand my role. The threshing machine
(or separator) is driven by a steam engine (this has 27 horsepower)
by means of a belt. On each side of the separator a wagon unloads
the sheaves into the machine. There were seven wagons here. Each
wagon has a teamster who steers the horses and unloads the wagon.
There were 4 pitchers. Our job was to load the sheaves onto the
wagons in the field, while the teamsters rode from one stook to the
other. When the wagon is full he goes to empty it into the machine,
while we go and load another empty wagon. There were 7 teamsters
and 4 pitchers, an engineer for the machine, a man who watches the
separator and regularly oils it, a tank man who gets the water for the
engine, a stoker, 3 or 4 men to transport the separated grain to the
granaries — in total we had about a 20-man gang. You can well
understand that wages take quite a bit of the farmer's harvest. The
teamsters and pitchers get the same wage, but an engineer gets $6 or
$7 per day and the separator man gets a dollar less than the engineer.
We threshed approximately 1200 bushels of wheat a day; the boss
gets 8 cents per bushel for wheat, 7 cents per bushel for oats, because it is easier to thresh, and 20 cents per bushel for flax.
At night we slept in a wooden shack, about three-quarters the size
of a bath house, lined with 8 bunks each capable of holding 2 men.
Everybody softened his bunk with some hay or straw, but it was
hard and stayed that way. These were rather strange surroundings for
me; in the middle of so many rough harvest hands in a 'caboose' you

could find every kind of person. In this gang were 2 Russian Jews, filthy dirty guys, too lazy to work, but they left rather quickly. There were 2 old men, about 55 I think, adventurers who had sought for luck their whole lives but had never found it. They were fellows who mentally converted their wages into whiskey. They talked of nothing else but whiskey and were unable to swallow their breakfast unless they had taken a shot to calm their empty stomachs. That's the way they all were, they worked (so to speak) for whiskey, that was their goal. Poor guys, and yet they could be completely different, they spoke of their past life, their homes, naturally interspersed with the necessary swear words, but one could sense a different mood. It often surprised me that they left me at peace.

When the work was finished I returned to Virden, and having nothing better to do I am waiting for my friend. Room and board at the hotel was $1.50 a day. I couldn't pay that so I took a room in a boardinghouse for $5 per week. If I have my choice I would go to the bush this winter with a friend and saw and chop trees. That's not so bad, it's hard work but you get thirty dollars per month and free board. Many people have advised me not to do it because the life is wild and woolly.

LUMSDEN, SASKATCHEWAN 22 JANUARY 1911

The farmer who hired us to drive his wheat was very disappointed
when his plans were frustrated by too much snow. And what did
that nice man do? The third day that we were there, I think, he told
us he couldn't use us and set us on the street, or as they say here, he
told us to 'clear out,' without saying a word about our wages. So
there we were with $11 between us. E. and I went to Regina, which
is 30 miles further west, and our first job there was to go to the employment office. E. was lucky and got himself a job as a farmhand in
Indian Head; nothing was left for me but to go and work on the
railroad.

And so now I'm working for the CPR, or rather for the contractor
to whom the CPR has granted the contract for laying the line. Perhaps it would be more correct to say that I'm working for the sub-
contractor who has taken over the laying of part of the line for the
contractor. I'm 15 miles from Lumsden, 20 miles north of Regina on
the Regina-Saskatchewan line. I work nine hours per day, 7-12 and
1-5 for 20 cents an hour, $1.80 per day and $10.80 per week. Five
dollars is taken off per week for board, so I'm left with $5.80 per
week. The job is pick work, loosening up pieces of rock and stone,
and loading the wagons, which the teamsters unload 3 miles from
here. You can understand that's not kid's work, but heavy labour.

My compatriots are a bunch of strong workers, used to this their
whole lives. We sleep in a caboose similar to that of threshing time, 8
bunks each holding two men. The majority of the inhabitants are
'Galicians,' by which one denotes Russians, Poles, Austrians, and
Ruthenians, one Luxemburger, and the rest Englishmen. I work in
camp 5, one of 9 camps in Lumsden, each separated by a couple of
miles, but all working together on the one project. It's been very
cold the last couple of days, 40 to 50 below, one day it was 60
below in the morning and 52 at noon. There was a violent snow-
storm which caused us to lose half a day, and we continually had to
watch each other's noses and cheeks to warn of the possibility of
frostbite. Sometimes half of a person's face is snow-white and then
you have to rub it vigorously with snow. I have to say that I'm keeping my end up, even if I do suffer from the cold. Sometimes I still
have cold feet, even with wearing 3 pair of warm winter socks, a pair
of sheepskin-lined moccasins, and over all that, elkskin moccasins.

To give you another example of the cold, you can't keep your hands warm in gloves, so you have to wear mitts, and it's extremely dangerous to take them off, even for a minute. It's mountainous around here, not like the Hartz or Norwegian mountains but like Valkenburg. The railroad runs around a lake surrounded by high mountains. It is supposed to be beautiful here in the summer, and a couple of rich Winnipeggers have built summer cottages around the lake, and they certainly know what they are doing. We are working on the top of the mountains, and besides the cold, we get an all too refreshing wind. The snow is very deep; you can sink up to your knees and deeper, and here and there are house-high snowdrifts. The food is good, and cook and cookie (helper) look after us well.

LUMSDEN, 29 JANUARY 1911

I imagined you writing in your own surroundings, and when I looked
up and looked around and saw my own surroundings — all those
lugubrious farmers' mugs, outcasts of society, gathered here in the
winter by lack of dollars — then just for a second a cold shiver went
through me.

The inhabitants of our camp are an underhanded bunch. The
Luxemburger is going to be cleared out this week, fired, as they say
here in the camp, because he's unsuitable for the work and lazy.
Four Galicians left during the week and tomorrow the other five are
going to leave. Then there will be four of us left, three Englishmen
and I. It will be a lot quieter then because the Galicians are all
mighty noise makers and fighters, crazy guys, but not as low and
mean and degenerate as the Englishmen. The Galicians love to make
music, the more noise the better. They can make an unbelieveable
amount of noise with a violin and a couple of harmonicas. The noise
just winds them right up and gets them in the mood to fight; very
dangerous fights sometimes. This week I saw a Galician attack an
Englishman from behind, he knocked him to the ground with one
blow from a pick. Believe it or not the victim survived, but he was
knocked unconscious. We have a fight every day, usually resulting
from a card game. This bunch is crazy about card playing and sometimes put as much as $3 on a card. Except for a few unpleasant oc-
currences I managed to steer clear of most of the trouble. I would
much rather associate with the Galicians than the mean, low, Englishmen; they are the nadir of degeneration, something like the
characters in Tolstoy's novels. The boss expects some other fellows
this week to replace the Galicians. Several more weeks and I'll be
leaving this railroad camp.

REGINA, 14th MARCH 1911

And now a short recounting of my wanderings since I left camp 5.
The camp was closed for two weeks and my check was only $3.70. I
earned more, but I bought several things in the store. I bought a pair
of buckskin moccasins because the elkskin moccasins, which I
bought in Winnipeg, weren't warm enough. I also received
deductions for a medical fee and livery.

I went to Regina with the hope that I would get a job on a farm
either around here or elsewhere. But the employment office had
absolutely no work to offer.

Finally men were asked for a camp. I was hired and the same day
went by train to camp 11, which is near Lumsden. I had survived
some difficult days. I hadn't eaten for 4 days. It's hard to believe the
things a person can withstand. When I arrived at the camp with 4
others, it was meal time, and you can understand that I fell to. I was
conscious of the danger of eating too much after a long fast but I
was so hungry, that in the evening my stomach gave me a lot of
trouble. However, the next morning the problem was gone and I
went to work with renewed spirits.

The inhabitants of the camp were divided into two groups. The
one group was moving earth. They were pushing the road through a
mountain, and moving the earth to lower areas, while the other
group kept busy moving rocks and stones. During the first week I
loaded wagons with earth using a shovel – that's no child's play.
You work from 6:30 to 12 and from 1 to 6 without a minute's rest,
not even time to blow your nose, and they've never heard of a coffee
break in Canada. After that week, one of the teamsters of the second
group was fired, and I asked the stable boss to give me his team. I
did satisfactory work, and so that second week I teamed a team of
mules.

The railroad contractors work only with mules because they are
much better suited for the work than horses. They can withstand the
cold and are much tougher than horses. During the fourteen days I
was there, two horses fell dead during their work, totally played
out. 'Played and frolicked to exhaustion,' says van Alphen, I think.

On the 26th of February all the camps were closed and work
stopped for a month. I had earned $10.66 during that period and so
was in pretty good shape, in that I could wait awhile until there was

work again. Yesterday, Monday, I got work here, looking after a
furnace which heats an apartment. It's an easy job, it doesn't pay
much, only $1.00 per day, but the room and board is included.
There are plenty of places on farms right now but I think I'll pass
them up to go to —'s at Yorkton.

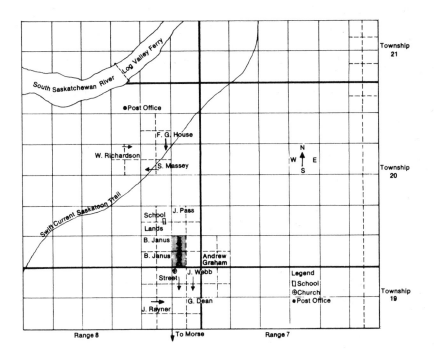

INDIAN HEAD, 6 AUGUST 1911

Now I'll give you a rough plan of the neighbourhood of my homestead. My half section is in 20:8 westerly half of 1 (as marked). G's
quarter is in the N.E. corner 19:8.25 (marked in black). The sections
marked through with a line (e.g. ◨) are all taken up and inhabit-
ed. In 20:8, 19 is the wood section (◼); it's about 6 miles from
my land. For 25 cents you can get a permit from the government to
cut wood in that section for firewood and lumber, that's one quarter
I think I will spend. Probably more land has been taken up in this
area than that which I've marked but that's all I can remember for
certain in my immediate neighbourhood.

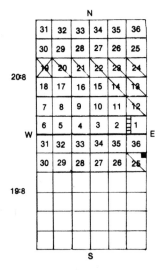

A couple of weeks ago we got a new hired hand on the farm, a
young Englishman who used to work for the W. family in the old
country. I'm talking about an Englishman, not a Scot or Irishman
because they're not English; the distinction is pretty sharply made
here.

The stuff in the garden is doing fine. We've been eating new
potatoes since mid-July, a good eating potato called 'the country
gentleman,' and a splendid cropper. We've had beans a couple of
times for dinner, and today we had peas for the first time. Pretty

soon the corn will be ripe and we'll really enjoy that, it's a real Canuck delicacy. A Canuck is a Canadian, a down-homer, a Londoner is a cockney, a green Englishman is a monsty, and an Indian is a nitchie. Today I washed a couple of shirts and saved 20 cents on laundry money. The Chinamen are unbelievably expensive, 10 cents apiece for a shirt, undershirt, or underpants, 5 cents for socks and 2½ for handkerchiefs.

MORSE, SASK., 10 NOVEMBER 1911

First a small letter to let you know what's happened to me since I left Indian Head Monday morning. Monday afternoon I arrived at Moose Jaw. Moose Jaw is 87 miles west of Indian Head, and Morse is 74 miles west of Moose Jaw, I had some business to complete at the Land Office there. I wanted to get a licence to cut some firewood in section 19 of my township, and I wanted to ask for some township plans for James. However, I was too late to get a turn, and so I went to Moose Jaw to spend the night, and try my luck the next day. Moose Jaw is a wild little town, not at all like Regina, which at least has a civilized gloss. It is especially busy right now because there are a lot of cowboys and farmhands spending their summer wages with abandon, and then looking for winter employment in the bush. No kidding, out of every ten people I saw, at least one was drunk. Needless to say there were plenty of fights and the lobbies of the hotels were full of drunken people.

In the morning I went to the Land Office and quickly completed my business. I couldn't leave for Morse until late in the evening because there were another couple of wrecks on the line. Nobody is surprised at this, because of all the wheat trains using the lines, train crashes are a common thing, but the railroad companies try to hush them up as much as possible. Late Tuesday night I arrived here at Morse and the hotel was packed to the rafters. Luckily I managed to get a place in a boarding house.

Wednesday morning, first thing, I went to the lumber office to get wood for my shack. I had estimated the amount of wood I would need, but I knew nothing about prices. The lumberman was an accommodating fellow; he corrected my estimate here and there, and advised me to do this and that in such and such a way. His estimate pleasantly surprised me, $36 for lumber, including a window and frame; I ordered my tarpaper from Eaton's and was surprised to find a letter from them at the post office with a cheque for $5.89. I had sent Eaton's a money order from Indian Head for $46.92 and I had enclosed $6 for freight. I figured that $6 would cover the freight, but he sent me the stuff and assumed the freight costs himself. All right Mr Eaton, if I ever need anything else, you can depend on my patronage!

I asked all about town, especially in the livery barns, if there was anybody around from the 20 miles North Settlement. But no luck, so I stayed here till this morning, Friday morning, and approached a lot of people to transport the lumber to my land, but all without success. Again and again a new disappointment. This morning I decided to walk to the settlement. I set out right after breakfast. Eight miles north I came to Mitchell's place and asked him about G. and all the other fellows. They all have to pass there if they go to town, because Mitchell's place is right on the road. But no, nobody was on his homestead, everybody had gone east or west with their oxen to bring in the harvest and do the threshing, and nobody had come back yet. Mitchell was prepared to help but not before Friday, 17 Nov., because he needed his own oxen to take his wheat and flax to town. On Friday he would be willing to take a load out to my homestead. So not being able to get help I returned to Morse. It was a cold trip, 22 below the whole day and a sharp west wind, which sometimes blew right in my face because the road is far from straight. A lot of snow has fallen here — it snowed continually — so that now there is a foot of snow. Once in a while it was difficult to see either the road or if I was still on the right track. Tomorrow I'm going to try the livery barns again, that will cost me more money, but it also costs money to stay in a hotel, $2 a day, and I want to put up my shack as quickly as possible. Who knows what the weather will be like in a couple of days, maybe colder and bleaker than now.

Morse is a prosperous little town. The Hudson Bay trail runs North-South, and where the CPR crosses it that's where Morse began. Four elevators, a hotel, post office, a doctor, even a notary public, 5 or 6 public stores, 2 restaurants, 2 hardware stores, 3 lumberyards, 3 bakeries — all together you can see they make up a nice town. A real Canadian town, even the traditional barbershops and poolrooms are to be found here.

They had a good crop here this year, number 2 and number 3 wheat, and a good flax crop, 12 to 14 bushels per acre. There were a couple of threshing outfits here and everybody's crop would have been threshed if the snow hadn't become a problem. The land north of town had a better crop than that which lies south. Tonight the hotel is full again, mostly homesteaders who are waiting for an acquaintance with a team to come and get them. There are some who live a hundred or more miles from Morse. I just talked to a Scotsman who has a homestead 125 miles south, and Morse is his nearest town. Have you got any idea what 125 miles means in the winter through a rough country, about 35 hours of travelling?

You can see the homesteaders leave town, just off the train, with oxen, horses, cows, calves, pigs, and their household goods, everything. You see them load up their wagons and move in bunches into the country for many, many miles. And the oxen go so slowly that you ask yourself if they will ever reach their destination. Northwards they trek, far over the Saskatchewan River and south close to the boundary, the builders of the Empire all right. You meet them here in the hotel, men of all nationalities and ages. Old men, who are giving it one more try, and young strong men who can take it. Swells and dandies talking about their homesteads with little cigars in their mouths. I don't think you ever see one of those swells survive a second winter on their homesteads. And next to them, you see others on whose faces you can read the resolution, ones who are frightened by nothing in this world and are determined. You can read the success on their faces.

Saturday morning. Just now I found a liveryman who will take me and my suitcase, and my load of lumber, out to the homestead Monday morning. Unfortunately my stuff from Eaton's hasn't arrived yet, maybe it will come today yet. But even if it isn't here by tomorrow night, I'm still planning to start. I hope I can find someone to help me build, and then at least I can raise the shack, even if I don't have Eaton's tarpaper to put between the double-boarding. The double-boarding is put up fast enough and I can get it when I go back into town for a load of coal.

13 NOVEMBER 1911

I am just going to go out to my homestead now with two loads, one of coal and another of lumber. The liveryman is driving me out for $25, pretty reasonable. Got provisions for a couple of months, a hundred-pound bag of flour, oatmeal, ham and beef, sugar, coal oil, etc. Bitterly cold, 20 below. Hope we are going to get some better weather yet, to give me a chance to put up my shack. Am wearing clogs on my feet, lumber-soled and felt-lined. It's a great rig, and they keep your feet warm in 30 below. I am wearing the two pairs of socks which you sent me, with paper between. Enjoyed a good sermon last night in the Presbyterian Church. We have two churches here.

30 NOVEMBER 1911

And now I'll go on with my story. I last wrote you from here about
16 days ago, telling you that G.D. and the other neighbours had not
yet returned from threshing and therefore could not deliver my
baggage. I also wrote you that I found a liveryman to load my goods
on two wagons and deliver it to the homestead. He had good
weather, it wasn't so terribly cold, but the road was poor and slippery, and it took us the whole day and part of the evening to reach
G.D.'s shack, where we stayed overnight. The next morning we
covered 1½ miles to my land and unloaded the goods. The teamster
tied the other team to the back of the wagon and returned to town.
I returned to G.D.'s where I was going to stay until I had everything
fixed up. And now I had to find some help to assist in building my
shack, and that wasn't easy. G. had just come home on Sunday and
had a lot of work to do for himself and the neighbours. So I merely
sat and waited patiently at G.'s. J.R. returned from threshing on
Saturday, and after much persuasion he agreed to help me for $3 per
day. Monday morning we began and by Wednesday evening the
shack was up, 12 foot long, 10 foot wide and 7 foot high. At G.'s I
pay $2 a week for board and that's as cheap as if I boarded myself.
Usually I go to the shack right after breakfast and fix up this or that,
and I also look around for the most suitable place to dig a well.
  I went to town today, not only to get the mail, but also to try
and hire a team for hauling firewood. On the way into town I visited
a German, at whose place we had stopped on Monday, 13 November, to eat dinner. He had told us then that he was pretty hard up
and that he had no money to see him through the winter. He didn't
want to rent out his oxen but he would come and work for me at
$2.50 per day. Friday and the following day we'll go and haul wood
from the bush in section 19 of the township. Five or six loads will
help me through the winter, I hope. That bush is 6 miles N.E. of my
place and we can manage to haul just one load per day.
  As far as the mail is concerned, if you don't pick up the letters
quickly (especially registered mail) they send it right back. As far as I
can understand they keep your mail at the post office for only 14
days, and if it hasn't been asked for, it is sent back.

ON THE HOMESTEAD 20 MILES ABOVE MORSE,
7 DECEMBER 1911

Nothing grows on alkali soil, absolutely nothing, not even weeds. The dimensions of my shack are 10 by 12 feet, and 7 feet high. The roof is a so-called car roof, bowed: from the side my shack looks like this ⌂ . Most of the shacks look like this ⌂ . I used two by sixes for the foundation (these are beams, stilts in English, 2 by 6 inches). The stilts lie on their edge, that is the 2-inch side on the ground and the 6-inch side up. Lying on the 4 outside stilts are the 2 by 4's, not on their edge, but with the 4-inch side on the two-inch side of the two by sixes. The studs (perpendicular beams) are nailed on the 4 two by fours. I used two by fours for the studs. These studs are perpendicular and stand at right angles to the foundation. There's a stud every 2 feet, so there are 6 on the 10-ft side, 7 on the 12-foot side, 22 in all. On top of these studs come the wall plates, also two by fours. I'll sketch one of the sides for you because the written description is terribly unclear, and you probably don't understand it at all.

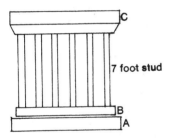

A   This is the 2 x 6 stilt.
B   is the 2 x 4.
C   is a wall plate, 2 x 4, it holds the studs in the right position.

This is one side of 4, and all are the same. This is the 10-ft. side, the 12-foot side has 7 stilts instead of 6.

This is the frame, now the planks. I used three kinds; ship-lap, drop-siding, and half-inch boards.

First ship-lap:
Cross-section
the planks fit
together like this:

And now drop-siding
Drop-siding fits
together like this:

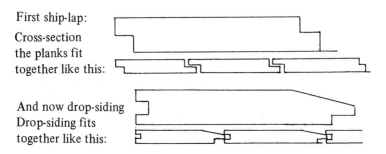

This is drawn at a bigger scale in order that the grooves can be drawn easier.

The boards are 6 inches wide and an inch thick. The half-inch boards were used for the roof and were 8 inches wide. When we had the frame up, all 4 sides as in the sketch, we wrapped 2 layers of tarpaper around it. Then we nailed the drop-siding on the studs. The next job was the floor, we used ship-lap here and for the double boarding inside. However, before we put up the double boarding we nailed wood stripping over the tarpaper, especially over the cracks of the laps. We did this in order to push the two layers of tarpaper together, and prevent the wind from blowing in. From the inside out the shack is made up of wood strips, tarpaper, and drop-siding. Now we got out the building paper and covered the inside of the shack, and used small nails to secure the building paper (two thickness) to the studs. Over this we nailed the ship-lap and over that another layer of building paper held in place by wood strips.

As far as the roof was concerned we put beams on top of the 7-foot frame to support it. In the middle we put a 2 by 8, 12-foot long, extending 1 foot on each end. On both sides we used a 2 by 6. We nailed the half-inch boards on these 3 beams and on the wall plates, so they are nailed on 5 beams. Then we nailed down two layers of tarpaper and on top of them another layer of half-inch boards, now the shack was finished.

You'll probably say that's a lot of paper. But they say paper is as good as a layer of wood, and it's much better at keeping the wind out. When I planned the construction of the shack I thought I had better make it as warm as possible because fuel is terribly expensive. I would build the best I could, and keep the heat in the shack and the wind out. And all those layers are not at all excessive. D. has 3 layers of paper and the wind still comes through on stormy days. His paper might not be as good as mine, but still, he has 3 layers. Everything considered the shack cost me close to $100. It's very difficult for me to say if I would advise or dissuade S. from coming to Canada. It's easy enough to make someone aware of the disadvantages, or to convince him of the fallacy of the 'land of milk and honey' idea, but what should you do, advise or dissuade? Surely a person has a chance to get ahead here, as he has nowhere else, but in order to get that chance, he has to say goodbye to an awful lot.

27th DECEMBER 1911

I've used my watch for a long time, but this spring I bought a dollar watch in Indian Head. The old watch was in poor condition and it fooled me by stopping every once in a while. I bought an Ingersoll watch and they certainly are a great rig. They are guaranteed to keep time for a year, and if they don't or you get any trouble with them in that year, you just wrap your watch in a piece of paper and send it to the factory. They repair it for nothing, or give you another watch. If something goes wrong after a year, they repair all the problems for 25 cents.

Today I took out a subscription for the *Free Press*, a Winnipeg paper. I plunked down a dollar for a whole year's subscription. As you can see your dollar can go quite a ways here. All paper and magazine subscriptions cost a dollar, and I will make sure that I get into town every week to pick them up.

All the ranchers along the river are butchering beef now for their own provisions, and they also butcher a little extra to sell to their neighbours. G. has his beef, as have Jim and Charlie, but not Tom. Tom will be going shortly and I'll go along and buy a quarter. The weight varies depending on whether you buy a front- or hind-quarter, as does the price, 9 cents per pound for front quarters and 11 cents per pound for the hind. The hind-quarter is the most desirable for a bachelor, because his chief utensil for cooking meat is the frying pan. A front-quarter is mostly boiling pieces, and a bachelor isn't much of a cook so he wants a roast. I've got a piece of pork upstairs but it is only a pound. Pork is really the best meat — it cooks the fastest and they claim that the fat keeps out the cold — but it costs 17 to 20 cents a pound, depending on the cut you take. I bought this piece at the butcher's in town. Buying meat here is a strange experience. You walk into a butchershop and see all the meat hanging: beef, pork, and mutton. The butcher gives you a knife or a saw and you cut off exactly what you want. Porkchops cost 20 cents a pound and side pork 17 cents. I took approximately 5 pounds of side pork, it's practically all fat, but it is ready in an instant and tastes delicious.

How's my cooking? That's going fine and you know I don't understand why people have to learn that art, either out of cook-books or at cooking school; there's really nothing to it. You simply

let everything cook until it's done and then you haul it out. You just
have to be careful that the stuff doesn't burn.

In the mornings I have a good breakfast; I cook oatmeal porridge,
eggs and bacon, (I use the fashionable 'eggs,' but usually it's the
singular: 35 cents per dozen). I have bread and tea, and for dessert,
bread and corn syrup or bread and peaches. That's all right, don't
you think? That stays with a fellow. Baking bread is also quite easy.
(The baker doesn't come to the door daily and I occasionally miss
the milkman.) I usually bake biscuits; they are a lot like 'cadetten.' I
can make about a dozen at a time in my baking pan in the oven.
(Drum oven from Eaton's, a dandy.) Every other day or so you have
fresh bread. You make them with flour, salt, and baking powder,
and if you have it, lard. (Lard is something like our 'reuzel,' I think.)
You can buy lard in tins at 20 cents a pound and you use it to make
your biscuits 'croquant,' as the French say. The price of flour varies
from 2 dollars to $3.35. The best flour is the easiest to handle, rises
easily, and bakes fast and good. As you would certainly expect in
this wheatland, we have 'great flour' which produces a healthy
nutritious loaf of bread.

It's cold at night in the shack after the stove has gone out. When I
get up in the mornings the thermometer is at 20 or 30 degrees below
zero. The last two days it was 35 below, and that's in the shack.
Quite a job to light the stove then, and build a fire, but once it's
started we soon drive out the frost. My stove'll help me, she's a
dandy.

2 FEBRUARY 1912

Around Morse things are pretty good, the ground is rich enough to
lose a little bit of its cream. You can have good paying crops here
when you get a dollar for a bushel of wheat (and that's number one),
and double for a bushel of flax. And because flax doesn't weigh
much more than wheat it's also easier to get to market, and that's
saying a lot when you live 20 miles from the elevators. When I was in
town the last time to get the coal, I talked to a homesteader who
had brought in a load of flax from his homestead, 65 miles south of
Morse. He had 36 bushels, and left his land Monday morning and
arrived in town Saturday evening. He'd been 'on the trail' the whole
week except for the Friday of the terrible blizzard, the one I wrote
you about. On his way to town he found the frozen body of a young
Scotsman who had set out early that morning to pick up his Christ-
mas mail in town. Within a mile of his shack he was confused by the
blizzard, he became lost, and walked around and around his shack in
a circle of a few hundred meters without ever finding it. Finally exhausted by his efforts he collapsed. That's how the blizzard claims
its victims. It's difficult to realize but you lose all sense of direction,
and you can be lost even though only a short distance from your
shack, because you can't see a half a yard ahead.

HOME, 17 FEBRUARY 1912

I'll tell you a little about the hotel in Morse. You don't see any class distinction here at all, and when the clock strikes 6 and the dining room doors opened, it's even more noticeable. There are six big tables in the dining room, each seating six men. The menu is very good: a choice of servings of soup, fish, roast meats, beefsteak, pork-chops, chicken, mutton, potatoes, vegetables, sweet pudding, tarts, fruit and cheese, tea, coffee, and chocolate. If you are hungry, you can take 3 or 4 meats, and if you prefer one over another kind you tell the girl 'quite a bit of pork.' So you say, 'soup, fish, roast beef, sirloin steak, mutton, and quite a bit of pork and tea.' The food comes in a wink of the eye and exactly what you ordered. It's quite a surprise to see that your fellow trenchermen have also ordered an immense amount, and that it all arrives at the same time as yours. The portions are not excessively large.

The menu for breakfast is as follows: porridge, cornflakes, grape-nuts, oranges, porkchops, beefsteak, ham and eggs, eggs as ordered (scrambled, poached, fried, boiled), pancakes, and fruit. Black tea, green tea, and cocoa. You usually begin breakfast with an orange, then you have cereal, meat and eggs, pancakes and stewed fruit (peaches, apples, or berries).

In most stores (they look like warehouses) you can get every-thing, groceries, clothes, shoes, hats, coats, everything but iron goods. You have to go to a hardware store for these. Generally you can get everything you ask for in a store, and get quick and amiable service, but you also have to pay a lot. In a restaurant you can get a good square meal for a quarter, and the Chinese are good cooks. Many 'so-called' permanent boarders live in the hotel. Bachelors who have business in town all live in the hotel. The doctor, minister, bank clerks, store clerks, elevator men, generally any bachelor who can pay the difference in price between the hotel and the boarding house. Practically everyone here is unmarried. Canada is the land of the bachelors, as there are very few women. You can get a haircut and a shave in a barbershop, haircut 35 cents and shave 15 cents. Yes, Canada is a good land, but getting rich overnight seems to be out of fashion.

The only bird which braves the winter is the snowbird. It's a small bird, a little bigger than an English sparrow, nicely marked with a snow white stomach and white wing edges. Yet there are not a lot; it's quite a rarity to see even a small flock of them. The badger doesn't sleep, but he's inactive and lazy and seldom leaves his hole. There seems to be enough of them here, if you figure by the number of holes you see, and feel, when you step into them after they've been covered by a layer of snow. There are quite a few wolves here; sometimes they go out in big packs, or a group of 5 or 6. They aren't dangerous and won't attack you when they are alone, and in a pack only if they are very hungry. You rarely hear that they have attacked a man; sometimes they do attack small children, terrible. We also have deer and antelope. You've probably heard that the antelope is the laziest animal and the white badger the most fashionable, but the antelope that I saw were really moving. I also found tracks around here of fox and mink, but I haven't seen any.

HOME, 23 FEBRUARY 1912

You'll also find a couple of pebbles in the package I sent you, I
found them while digging my well. I'm very curious to hear what
those pebbles are since they look a lot like gold. Not that I think
that I've found gold, but Jim said that it does resemble it an awful
lot. I found a couple of big rocks and knocked these chunks off with
the pick. Canada is a strange country and you can expect anything.
A couple of weeks ago they found gold in the Duck Mountains of
Manitoba. Immediately there was a tremendous rush and over 3000
claims were staked. The experts, however, declared that the gold
wasn't present in paying quantities, and with that sad news the
majority of fortune seekers went on their way. You shouldn't think
of me as being foolish enough to speculate on gold; 'honest toil' is
my speculation.

Speaking of my well, I dug 200 yards South of my shack, at the
foot of the hill upon which my shack rises so majestically. It is quite
a job just to get through the frost, which is not less than 4 feet deep.
Just like rock! I've managed to dig down 7 feet and it is very difficult to throw up the earth now. So I'm waiting for a helper, either
Jim or Charlie, to haul up the earth which I've dug. It's pleasant
work when you know that you earn yourself 75 cents for every foot
you dig. It doesn't go very fast because the ground is so hard, but
you know that every blow of your pick brings you one step closer to
your goal, until finally you reach water. It's just like that with a trip
to Morse, every step forward brings you nearer, 'no hand can hold
you down.' I talked about getting a helper, Jim and Charlie are kind
of well experts and they'll give me a hand. I hope to reach water at
12 or 14 feet. At present I'm still melting snow; that's a real job and
it keeps you busy. Snow is only ¼ to a ⅓ water and fresh-fallen
snow is even less.

As soon as the stove is out in the shack it freezes till it cracks. In
the morning everything has to be unthawed, the bread is as hard as a
stone. I eat a lot of meat but fairly irregularly. Sometimes I eat 2 or
3 pounds per day and then I live on bread and beans and no meat. I
don't know yet where I shall go to in the spring, but there will probably be good wages as there is a lot of threshing to do yet this year.

HOME, 29 FEBRUARY 1912

In December I bought 5 dozen eggs in town and I still have 2 dozen left. They are frozen, but as long as they stay frozen they'll be all right. If you break the shell you find a clump of ice. There is only one way to unthaw them and that is to lay them in the snow that you're melting on the stove. That's the only way. If you lay them in warm water or try to unthaw them in any other fashion the egg white will unthaw but not the yolk. At sunset in the winter we often see 'sundogs,' they're something like rainbows except that they don't signify rain and aren't bows. You'll probably say that it doesn't leave much of a rainbow, just the colours. You see, the sun is about a yard or so above the horizon flanked by perpendicular rainbows. It's surely a sign of cold. I never saw one in Holland and never heard of one before, except in Canada.

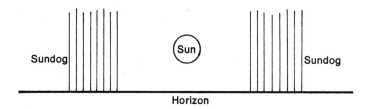

I saw Billie H.'s oxen. I haven't told you about that yet. I think I wrote you a few words about my visit but not the reasons for it. Billie gets the patent for his homestead this spring and becomes the legal owner, but he prefers to work in the city so he is going to quit farming. He's selling his outfit now, six good oxen, the best I've seen up to now. First I have to tell you that if you buy oxen in winter you can usually get them either without a cash down payment or a very small one. However, if you buy them in the spring or summer you usually have to pay half in cash and the balance in 1 or 2 Falls. I thought to myself, buy 2 or 3 oxen in the winter and you can work them to pay for their feed. Charlie had hay for sale, one ton for an acre of breaking or 4 dollars cash. One ton feeds a team easily for a month, and they could easily earn that 4 dollars by hauling wood from the bush, or on other jobs like riding grain to town for the people from across the river. I saw Billie's oxen, beautiful animals in mint condition. He really wants to sell all six together, with harness and a 2-furrow plow (a John Deere gang plow) for $750. I picked out, so I thought, three of the best and he asked $340. For a team of 2, No. 1 and 2 combined, he asked $210 and for 2 and 3 combined he asked $275 dollars. At that price they weren't expensive at all, but he wants half in cash and the other half in the fall, so at that stage our negotiations fell through. He said that in the spring he would probably ask $15 or $20 more per ox, but we'll see.

My neighbours have all bought their seed and so each will have a crop this year, mostly flax but also some wheat and oats. Flax is the best crop for a homesteader; it depletes the land somewhat, but it gives him some working capital. Jim and Charlie bought 10 bushels of flax together ($1.75 per bushel). They each hope to have 10 acres in crop. Jim only has 5 acres of his land broken, but Charlie will help him in the early spring to break 5 more, and then he will break 10 acres for himself. They'll be sowing 15 acres of just broken land, that's all right for flax, but not as good for wheat. Potatoes also do fine on new breaking! Say you get 10 or 12 bushels per acre (which is not a lot), that gives you about 100 bushels of flax, and take an average sale price of $1.75, that gives you $175. Even if you only get a hundred it's still pretty nice. George is sowing flax, Tom wheat.

HOME, 8 MARCH 1912
NOTEWORTHY.

In Strathmore, one of the adjacent towns, there is even a Dutch settlement. All the Hollanders that Janus met in Calgary and Vancouver
mourned their departure from Holland. Most of them had come here
with a good stake, and had invested it in land which they could now
probably sell for only half of their investment. The whole settlement
at Strathmore was brought here by a priest. He was engaged and paid
by the CPR to give lectures in Holland (especially Brabant), and to
lure these people out to the so-called 'irrigated farms' belonging to
the CPR. When he had lured these people out here, he got so nervous
that he took off.

I can't advise people enough, especially those who are coming
here, to be careful, get the lay of the land first. As far as baggage is
concerned, wear a good strong travelling suit but don't bring work
pants and such. Wear a good pair of stout shoes but don't buy anything special. Bring a good bundle of dollars, they'll be of more use
than clothes. Don't buy a railway ticket in Holland because they will
cheat you. If you show your immigration card at the station
wicket — you'll get that at the landing of your boat — you'll get a
much lower fare. Buy a ticket for Winnipeg and go on your own;
don't travel with the Salvation Army. When you arrive at Winnipeg
go to the Dominion Land Office and ask for a job on a farm in the
vicinity of Regina, on the CPR line, preferably a few stations west of
Regina, Qu'Appelle, Indian Head, or Pilot Butte. At the land office
you can hear a lot about your future boss, if he's married and has
children how much land he has and how many horses. Go to work
on a large farm where there are other hired hands. As soon as you
land, lay aside your differences, be more or less impudent and trust
no one, regardless of the good advice that is given you. Furthermore
travel 2nd class because you'll get through the immigration control
easier and you will be treated more courteously. One more good
piece of advice, talk English with everyone, even amongst yourselves,
forget your Dutch. Introduce yourself to everyone and talk with
them, but don't believe anything about Canada until you have seen
it with your own eyes.

HOME, LOG VALLEY, 15 MARCH 1912

Burrill was no homesteader even though Elgin was founded by home-steaders. Burrill's landlord had acquired the farm by homesteading. He was 60 miles from town, there was no Elgin then, and his nearest market for grain was Brandon. Practically everyone who had ac-quired his farm by homesteading rented his land out and lived in Elgin, or had bought land in another area. You probably ask why. Well, all that land was exhausted by the overcropping carried out by the old pioneers. Years ago, they didn't consider the relation of summerfallow to fertile land. Elgin had good crop years, as did all of Manitoba, but now it's finished. An average crop of 20 bushels is nice, it's beautiful for Manitoba. In Saskatchewan they get a much higher average and they'll keep it, thanks to the better system of agriculture. Still, once in a while, you did find a pioneer who had stayed on his old homestead.

Water lay deep in Elgin. If I'm not mistaken it was at 85 feet at B.'s. Generally water is a pretty scarce commodity in America; not only in Canada, but also in the States, the lack of it can cause quite a bit of trouble. For example, here in West Saskatchewan you have the Gooselake Country, a beautiful district for wheat. They get great crops but there's no water; the water has to be hauled in from 10 to 20 miles away. Because of the scarcity of water it's almost im-possible to keep horses or cattle, for that matter the work is mostly done by gasoline engines. The prairie is said to be totally brown there and there's neither water nor hay for the cattle. And when it does rain, the quantity is practically minimal.

Practically everyone suffers from bad teeth and they usually blame it on the water. Because of this state of affairs the area is crawling with dentists, there's at least one in every town. A good-paying job in this country. A township is not a municipality; you could probably compare it to section A, B, and C in Holland. There's a mayor and council in Morse, all farmers naturally. Those positions haven't evolved into permanent ones yet. What kind of trees do we have here? We have poplar (black and green), the red willow and occasional ash and maple tree, but the poplar is the most common. They experimented with fruit trees at the Forestry station at Indian Head but without much success. They got some fruit but it was tasteless, and there was very little of it.

HOME, 28 MARCH 1912

I have subscriptions for the *Weekly Free Press* and the *Prairie Farmer* at a dollar each. Every paper costs a dollar per year here; the reason for the low price lies in the fact that they are delivered postage free, no franking costs, so practically everyone gets a good selection of papers. And you certainly get something for your money, if not in news, then certainly in paper. A couple of weeks ago one of the articles dealt with the changes occurring in people since they had moved to America. Someone had noticed that the brain-pan (craniums) of many Russians and Galicians had changed, more than would naturally have been expected in their descendants. I have noticed a change in my blood. When I came here I had thick dark red blood, but now, after my first winter here, I have very thin light red blood. I remember that they told me in Elgin that I wouldn't feel the cold as much in my first winter because I would still have my 'Old Country' blood.

Spring is now busy trying to become a fact. It's unbelievable what a couple of days, as we had after Saturday, can do. The snow is practically all gone — here and there there is some left over from the winter, snowdrifts — but generally the snow has all disappeared. Even the winds, the spring winds, have come and quickly dry up the water which doesn't have time to sink into the ground. And now we have clouds again, clouds of evaporated snow; they had practically disappeared during the winter. Luckily my well is down and there's 8 or 9 feet of water in it. The water isn't very clear yet, but it's water anyway, and it will slowly clear up. I plan to line the sides with planks, this stops the earth from falling in, but I'll need 300 feet of lumber or $9, and I could use that to buy a pump. I built an artificial snowdrift on the south side of my shack this winter. I put up a structure of poles to catch the snow, and so I had plenty of water from the drift the whole winter.

This morning Janus and I permanently established the borders of our land. We set the border for the whole mile along the North side. North of us is section 11, the school section. In every township 11 and 29 are the school sections. If there are 12 or more school age children in a neighbourhood the government sells the school section by public sale and places the money in a trust fund. This money is used to build and support the school. Furthermore, everyone is required to pay a school tax whether he has children or not — that doesn't matter in the least — and everyone pays the same amount. The amount of the tax therefore depends in great part upon the price which the school section brings at the sale. Sections 8 and 26 in every township belong to the Hudson's Bay Company; this company was to Canada what the East Indian Company was to our East. Furthermore, as recompense for building the line from Winnipeg to the coast, the CPR received from the government all the odd sections in a township, which either bordered on the line or through which the line ran. Thus they received sections 1, 3, 5, 7, 9, 13 etc.

We read the advertisement in the *Nieuws* about the lectures to be given by Mr Boer, the retired inspector of the CPR water works, those so-called 'irrigated farms.' What a swindle. Janus was there and met dozens of Hollanders who had walked into the trap. They were fleeced by a priest who got so scared that he took to his heels. Believe me, those guys get a good salary from the CPR. I could go to the government too, and recruit Hollanders in Holland for emigration to Canada. They would pay me in land, so much land for so many wealthy Hollanders.

HOME, 13 APRIL 1912

In the last couple of weeks, the strong spring winds together with
the warm sun have made everything cork dry. Practically every day,
and certainly every evening, we saw fires all around us on the
horizon, prairie fires. Some were miles and miles away, others close
by. Many evenings we sat and worried, because a fire with a strong
wind in back can move unbelievably fast. We had begun to burn a
firebreak around the shack, but this dangerous work could only be
done on windless evenings, and even then it was very dangerous. In
three evenings we had gotten as far as burning firebreaks on two
sides of the shack, the North and West sides. We were protected on
two sides by a fire guard 8 yards wide; we thought this would protect us from any future prairie fires. Wednesday, Thursday, and
Friday we were prevented from burning our firebreak further by a
continuous high wind.

    Wednesday evening we saw a fire which was dozens of miles from
us, but we saw it was moving at a terrific speed. We stayed up late,
but when we saw very little change in the fire glow we went to bed.
For the sake of security we let the alarm clock ring every hour so we
could keep an eye on the fire. It was all right, we made it through
the night, and by daybreak we couldn't even see the rosy glow. So
Thursday morning everything looked OK, even though the high wind
was still blowing with a good force. Janus had several letters to mail
and so he set out for the post office. After Janus had been gone
about an hour and I was busy baking bread and doing the wash, I
suddenly saw flames within a mile of my shack. The wind was still
from the south-east, but the flames could possibly eat into the wind
and then I would be done for.

    Janus had seen the fire coming and had turned back at Steven's.
He managed to get through the fire, which had crossed our trail, and
he reached the shack all right. He had seen the fire close up, helped
Steven to put out some flames, and saw the fire eating its way into
the wind and recognized the danger we were in. Right away we
began a backfire. It was dangerous, but it was sink or swim, and if
we didn't have a firebreak on all sides, all our possessions would be
gone in 20 minutes. So everything was at stake. Luckily, at the
bottom of the hill on which my shack stands, there is a low spot
with lots of water in it. Quickly we filled a tub and a boiler with

water. We touched the grass with a match and the wind whipped up
the fire, and faster than it takes me to tell you this, the fire had
sprung towards the shack. It took all our might to get the fire out in
time. Now we had to do the south-west side yet. I saw that we had
to have quicker method to put out the flames, so I ran into the
shack, grabbed a blanket which I quickly dipped into the pool of
water and sped back up the hill. Janus apparently had not noticed my
absence and had begun a backfire on the unprotected side. But he
couldn't manage the flames alone, they simply sprang up the hillside
and surprised us by becoming one great fire. He yelled to me, and I
ran halfway up the hill with my wet blanket, I went to work like a
madman, and thanks to the wet blanket we managed to smother the
flames a yard from the shack. We had made it.

We now saw the flames roll around us. They couldn't spring over
the north fireguard, so with roaring speed the flames moved to the
North-west, and west and slowly but surely they ate their way into
the wind to the south. Here and there around the shack, one thing or
another was still smoking, but these were easily put out with the wet
blanket. I stayed around the shack because I didn't dare leave it yet,
but Janus went ahead to help Bert Street. There was lots of time
because the fire crept slowly southwards. Bert Street doesn't have a
plowed fireguard around his shack either.

Over the road, and a half mile dead east of his shack, is Jack
Webb's newly built lumber stable and his partially erected shack.
Only the frame is up and all the other wood is piled on the ground,
with no firebreak around it. Janus hurried to Jack Webb's property;
Jack had just come along that morning with George Dean. Janus
managed to burn a fireguard and he only had a wet bag as an ex-
tinguisher. And I have to admit that he did a tremendous job; he
saved both the stable and the shack. I went over to Bert Street's
shack, where he and his wife were carrying water and sprinkling the
ground; this was useless as the strong wind dried it right up. We then
started a backfire. Street was afraid that the whole business would
burn up, but when I explained to him how we had managed to save
my shack all alone, he let me proceed. All three of us, Street, his
wife, and I were prepared to jump to with wet blankets and tubs of
water. We had burned a good fireguard on three sides when the fire
suddenly surprised us; it attacked on our weakest side and stormed
up the hill with so much power that I thought we would have to give

up. But with unbelievable speed and skill we managed to master the
situation again. We had depended upon the other three sides but in
two places the fire had blown over and was licking against the shack.
We also managed to get this under control and out. We managed to
master the situation pretty nicely here; the only damaged shack was
that of George House, and his hay stacks burned as well. I don't
know how the oxen will be fed this year; the only prairie grass is in
the low places where there was water. It takes 2 or 3 years before
the grass reaches any length at all. Strange, first the prairie was
white, then yellow brown, and now pitch black.

HOME, 30 APRIL 1912

Every rancher, and also most farmers who have stock, brand each
animal with their own brand. The different brands are registered
with the government, and any animal carrying a brand can be claim-
ed anywhere by the owner. Joe Williamson has a brand: ⋏ . In
the spring he bought some cattle and we branded them all. Other
brands are ✗ , ⋉ , ℒℬ etc. ℒℬ is a brand you see quite
often as it belongs to a horse ranch at Maple Creek. Every year at the
two round-ups, spring and fall, all the ranchers in the neighbourhood
drive the stock together and pick out their own cattle by the brands.
Sometimes their cattle get lost in another person's bunch.
    If a ranch sells cattle a horizontal line is burnt under the brand,
✗̲ . The buyer burns his brand, if he had one, under the old one $\frac{X}{\cancel{\text{LB}}}$.
This indicates that ✗ brand has sold the animal to ℒℬ .
Normally the brand is on the left side on the hind-quarter, but
sometimes, like the ℒℬ brand, it is found on the front leg.
    I think I wrote you in an earlier letter than I had a visit from
Andrew Bryce; a fellow who lives east of us. He needed a man and
came to ask me to work for him. I told him then that I preferred to
sit out my time first before leaving the homestead. I told him that
my time was over on the 8th of May, and that he should let me hear
something from him if he hadn't found a hired man by then. Just
this morning he came visiting in his buggy and asked me. 'Well sir,
How's chances?' I said, 'Pretty fair, tie your stud up somewhere
around here, come in, and let's talk it over.' And so we talked it over
and I've hired myself out to him for 4 months. In the fall I plan to
go out threshing with a team of oxen and a wagon, I believe I will be
able to earn more money than if I had hired myself out for the 6
months till freeze-up. He wasn't particularly happy about my deci-
sion, but when he saw that I would hold my position, he said, 'All
right then.' He expects me on his farm on Tuesday evening, 7th of
May, that's just over a week from now. The main reason I took this
job was to find out how to make this land as productive as possible.
There are other reasons for taking the job, loneliness, the fact that
I'm his first hired hand, and last but not least, that I will alternate
working for him one week and his brother for one week. His brother
lives 3 miles from his place. Bryce is a Canadian, a fellow from down
east. They are not particularly known as good bosses. I've been hired

as a teamster for 4 horses to break land, plow stubble, sow flax, disc, and harrow. He works the horses in tandem, in double Indian file, like this xx
           xx
            o   x=horse, o=equipment and driver.

The usual manner is all abreast: xxxx
                                     o

    I've never handled horses in this fashion and have never seen anyone else do it; I only read about it, and then only that this was a less successful method. Well, I'll learn about it from close-up; it will be a little strange at first but I think I'll get used to it. Bryce, his father, and 4 other brothers all have homesteads a couple of miles from each other. They took them up about 5 years ago and are now getting ahead fairly well. Two brothers got together this year and bought a gasoline engine for plowing and threshing their own grain. Bryce lives in section 34, township 21, range 7, so he lives about 12 miles, as the crow flies, from my place. Here's a sketch of four townships.

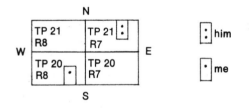

He's a councillor for his township and his post office is in Brycetown, named after the Bryce family, 4 miles from his homestead. All that's there is the post office; it's not a town and there are no stores. Mail comes twice a week.

BRYCETOWN, 23 JUNE 1912

Well, we got through a hot week. The temperature was about 100 degrees in the shade the whole week, and today we reached 105 at one o'clock. This morning we heard the first sermon in the new church. There were so many people that the church seemed almost too small to hold them all. We had another beautiful sermon by our preacher, Mr Slower. A couple of pails of water stood at the door and it wasn't long before all the water was gone. It was terrifically hot in the church and everyone was sweating like a bull. This whole week I've been breaking for Alex, and it's getting hard work now, as the sod is getting pretty tough. Friday I went to town with Alex, to Bridgeford; he took the tank to get oil for the engine and I took 75 bushels of wheat. The roads were good, but just the same it's a hard trip on the horses, they sweat an awful lot and they're not used to travel on the roads. We had a bit of thunderstorm this afternoon, a few drops of rain fell and that made it a lot cooler. The crops could do with a little rain too, though I must say, the prospects are as good as they ever were. The wheat is about 6 to 8 inches high and the flax is coming up nicely too. The mosquitoes are a proper plague all right and they are a hard thing to get used to, though there are not quite as many as there were a couple of weeks ago.

HOME AGAIN, 19th JULY 1912

I've had some unpleasantness again with Alex, enough to make me quit. I told you in an earlier letter that we had some argument over the meals when we went on our trip to Bridgeford. This time he came up with a new wrinkle. Last night he told me that he was going to town today, with two wagons, he would drive one and tie the other horse and wagon on the back. 'And what are you going to do with Bill?' I asked. 'Well,' he said, 'I guess you could do some hoeing in the garden till I come back.' And then I blew up, naturally! He was going to town with two teams to save the cost of my meals, and so he was going to turn me into his garden to hoe for two days. 'Tomorrow morning I'm leaving and I don't care to work for a fellow with those ambitions!' Now, that he hadn't expected, he knew he had a high card but he hadn't expected me to throw my hand down.

The first thing he said then was about my wages. You have to understand that if you are hired for a certain period of time, and you quit without good reason before your time is gone, that you are not entitled to even one cent. He said he was not going to pay me any wages, that means a half-month's wages to me. I've worked two months for the brothers, but because I agreed to work the first month on trial, I'm only entitled to one month's wages and this is supposed to be shared by Alex and Andrew. So Alex owes me a half month's wages. I have no idea what will happen with Andrew. I'm supposed to go back to work for him on Monday. But in any case, it's dawned on me that the brothers have discussed this possibility. This I understand very well, that they felt very safe with regard to a man to whom they owed a month's wages, and they knew that he couldn't demand them when he left. There is a sort of an agreement here, in judicial terms it's called a 'natural contract or agreement,' you are entitled to the money but you cannot bring a lawsuit or action. You ought to know that in every hamlet there's a jury which makes decisions regarding disputes between farmers and farmhands. If I don't get my wages willingly I'll go to the jury. And I ought to also tell you that a hired man is presumed to be within his rights, and the fact that I was hired as a teamster also aids my position. Alex was pretty inconvenienced, harvestime is drawing near and it's a difficult job to get enough men, especially so far from the railroad.

They don't like to go any farther from town than necessary, and the harvesters don't like to get too far from their whiskey.

Just now I had a visit from Mr Eliott, a young Irishman. Since last month he's held church at Steven's every other Sunday. Janus is a great admirer of his. He told me last time I was here that he had heard his sermon with great pleasure. In order to make things easier for us, he will preach twice on Sunday, 3 o'clock in the afternoon in the Street's shack and 7 o'clock in the evening at Massey's. A prairie minister like that is a completely different person than an 'Old Country' minister.

Jim Raynor returned with two oxen, which he bought on the condition that he would work for the seller this summer and earn them in that way. He is now busy breaking with his two oxen and Janus' two. The crops around here look good, thanks to the abundance of rain. The land is only roughly worked, and only with a lot of rain can you expect a moderate crop. The breaking done in the spring of last year has been disced and harrowed; this should have been done in the summer and fall of last year. They didn't have a proper seedbed and the soil can't preserve the moisture, but the crops will be all right, as long as they get lots of rain. I'm planning to have my 8 acres of broken land worked, so that I can have my land ready for seed this spring. I want to get it done properly; I'll have it double-disced and double-harrowed, and I expect it will cost me $1.50 per acre.

HOME, 16 AUGUST 1912

It's ten-thirty Friday morning and it's raining, not a cloudburst, but
a steady soaking rain. And that's the way it's been practically the
whole week. It's quite a disappointment for us as we had expected
to stack quite a bit of hay. Janus went to town last week and bought
a wagon, a mowing machine, and a rake, and when I got home last
Sunday he had cut quite a bit of hay. But as I said, the weather was
very un-co-operative this week. It rained Monday, Tuesday, and
Wednesday; Thursday there seemed to be a change in the weather.
Wednesday night we had a little bit of rain, but Thursday morning
the sun peeked through once in a while. There was a brisk breeze
and we hoped that the hay would dry enough in the morning so we
could begin to stack it in the afternoon. And it did dry very well.
The hay, which Janus had raked into piles, was dry on top but a
little damp underneath, so right after dinner we went to work and
turned the piles over. When we were finished at 4, the hay was dry,
we yoked the oxen to the wagon, and hauled two big loads which we
stacked west of my shack. The stack was 100 yards from the shack,
next to an auxiliary stable which I had built for the oxen out of
poplar poles. When we had loaded half of the third load the sky
clouded over and it started to rain again. It rained the whole night,
and today it rained again.

You are probably wondering how the Dickens we can make hay
after this spring's prairie fire. Well, we don't cut grass on the prairie,
but in the sloughs. Sloughs are something like marshes and some are
over an acre in area. These sloughs retain their water for quite a
while, but if they are broken up they are exactly like ordinary land.
This slough grass is beautiful this year, thanks to the abundant rain,
in some places it's 3- or 4-foot high. Even though there isn't as
much nourishment in it as in prairie grass or 'prairie-wool,' the
animals like it much better. You can cut 10 loads of slough grass as
easily as 2 or 3 loads of prairie wool. If the weather is a little bit
co-operative, we hope to stack over 100 tons for sale (2000 pounds
is one ton); this is excluding enough for our own use (the animals'
that is). We each hope to make a couple of hundred dollars on the
deal.

HOME, 14 SEPTEMBER 1912

Monday morning I went to town with the oxen to stock up on groceries, and at the same time to get some wood for a hay rack. That's quite a trip, 20 miles with oxen. They went very slowly but we arrived at Morse at 6 o'clock. My stomach growled with hunger, so my first job was to get supper at Charlie the Chinaman's. I just left the oxen standing in front of the restaurant. After sunset I drove the oxen and wagon about 1½ miles outside of town and camped for the night. I could have stayed in a bed overnight in Morse, and put the oxen in a stable, but I didn't dare to do it because they will steal anything in Morse. It was a cold night on the open prairie, and without blankets. But in any case, when it got light I yoked the oxen to the wagon and went back to town to finish my business. Tuesday I finished my business at the bank, bought groceries and lumber, and by 4 o'clock, having finished my business, I left town. It was exceedingly busy in Morse; with the harvest all the stores are full and you can hardly get into the lumber yard. Tuesday evening, about 8 o'clock, I reached the lake 10 miles from town, unyoked the oxen, and camped for the night. Wednesday morning at 10 I reached home. Janus and I quickly set to work to build the hay rack and almost finished it by evening.

Monday, Tuesday, and Wednesday were beautiful days, and there suddenly seemed to be a change in the weather after 6 wet weeks. Naturally we hoped to be able to pile all our hay. Thursday we christened our new rack and hauled 4 loads, then the sky clouded over and it began to rain again. Yesterday the same tune, and today we had rain again. We've decided to remain here until the end of this month and then go out alone. Our roving expedition will probably last until November, but before we leave we have to build a stable for the oxen for this winter. We also have to do more work on Janus' sod house and I have to fence 10 acres of pasture for him.

LOG VALLEY, 12 OCTOBER

We were very busy last week, we finished Janus' sod house, did our
road work, built a sod stable for the oxen for the winter, and stacked ten loads of hay. Exactly as anticipated, we were finished by
Saturday evening. Sunday afternoon Janus left with the wagon and
oxen to go to a threshing outfit which is working about six miles
east of here. He earns $5 per day, of which I get 1½ dollars for my
team. Harvesting wages are about 5 dollars for team and man, and 3
dollars per day for a man without a team. Janus earns $3.50 for his
wagon, because the wagon is his. Luckily we also finished his house;
when he returns he can crawl right into it.

What a job that is, building a sodhouse, but once it's finished it's
naturally a lot warmer in winter and cooler in summer than a
wooden shack. Still it's too bad that he was so pig-headed about the
construction — he knew everything better than anyone else — but
that's why it's a 'poor job' and a weak building. The roof construction is especially unfortunate, and he'll lose a lot of heat that way
this winter. Furthermore, he built it way too high, the walls are at
least 8 feet high, with the result that in the middle, the walls sag
towards the outside. I now have a neat and warm sod stable for the
oxen, a frame of poplar poles inside and sods piled against them on
the outside. Building with sod has the advantage that it's warm in
the winter and cool in the summer, and the sod doesn't cost anything. There are disadvantages however; it's a lot of work, and if you
figure your time and that of your oxen, then it's more expensive
than building a wooden house or stable. When Janus began to build
his shack he hired our neighbour to the East. He paid him $12 to
haul sod, from the place they were ploughed up, to the shack. And
for this $12 he had only about a third of the rquired sod that he
needed for the whole building. If he hadn't been able to use my
oxen, then the shack would have run him into a lot of money.

As I already told you, we did our road work last week. This is the
way that goes. We have to pay taxes, $8.80 per ¼ section yearly, so
$17.60 for a ½ section. Now they'll let you work out $9 and then
you have to pay $8.60 cash. If you want to earn the $9 yourself you
tell the road master; he tells you what work he wants you to do for
this sum. He ordered Janus and me to plow a road between our half
section. Stephen Massey lent us his sulky plow and two oxen on

Thursday. Together with my two oxen we had enough to pull the plow, and so we did our road work and earned $18.

As I mentioned before, Janus left Sunday afternoon with the oxen, accompanied by Jack Webb and Charlie Raynor and their oxen, all of them were going to work for the same outfit. This outfit is now East of us and will also thresh our settlement, but he's got 2 or 3 weeks of good solid threshing before he reaches us. Unfortunately, he just had a breakdown with his machine, so they couldn't work on the gang either Monday or today, and so they had to hang around empty. I wrote you that I also planned to go out threshing, but Steven asked me to come and work for him for a couple of days at $3 per day. He wants me to help him stack hay. He's anticipating an early winter, the coming of snow, and the impossibility of threshing until the spring comes. The grain naturally suffers much less in a stack than if it remains unstacked. So I've been working for Steven these last two days and have 6 little dollars in my swag. He's evaluating all the prospects, if things look rosy − and the possibility of this harvest being threshed now is greater than the possibility of it being threshed this spring − he won't stack everything, only a part.

When I'm finished at Steven's, maybe in a few days or maybe in two weeks, I'll go straight to working on a threshing machine. There is plenty of work to find around here at $3 a day. They are always short of men and people with threshing outfits ride through the country practically begging you to come to work for them. Almost certainly the wages will go higher next week; across the river there is an outfit that pays $4 per day and $6 for a team. Since the middle of last week we've had good weather, beautiful weather. If it stays that way for another couple of weeks then we can really earn some money, and that always comes in handy.

Beautiful weather again today, that makes it so much nicer to work than that cold, misty, wet weather of which we've had so much lately. Now I wanted to tell you something about our railroad, the Grand Trunk Pacific line from Watrous to Swift Current. Our chances are, and remain, pretty good, in fact are getting better. The first survey ran 3 miles North of Steven's place. Now they've changed the survey and it goes right in front of Steven's house. Four big tents, a sleeping tent, a cook tent, a tent for the boss of the survey crew, and another sleeping tent make up the accommodations.

In total there are 20 men with 3 teams of horses. They've camped here for 3 weeks and next week they'll trek further West with their camp. The development of a railway line costs a tremendous amount of money, the 20 men average $50 per month each in wages, then the three teamsters, the boss gets $150, the cooks get $60 and their board is free. They've been busy on this line since April and they don't figure on finishing before January or February. I might be able to get a job with the outfit for the months of Oct., Nov., Dec., and Jan., at $40 per month.

LOG VALLEY, 10 NOVEMBER 1912

We began to thresh Friday the first of November. They had quite a
job getting the machine here from town, and we've had several small
breakdowns which have stopped the threshing. It's slow going but
the work is progressing. Then we have some rain, some snow, and
the work is stopped for another half or whole day. And then sometimes a screw, a grating, or a key on the engine comes loose and
holds us up for an hour or so. When it began to snow Saturday afternoon, we had threshed 10 acres of flax for Charlie and 10 for Jim
Raynor: 70 acres for Tom Potts (wheat, oats, flax, and barley), 20
acres apiece for George Dean and John Kerr, and we were busy
threshing 30 acres of flax for Billy. It snowed last night and this
morning, but this afternoon it's melting again. If it doesn't snow
tonight we'll probably get to work again tomorrow afternoon. It's
unpleasant harvesting weather, wet, miserable, and as cold as the
Dickens, especially at night. And you really feel the cold then, because you're sleeping under open skies and there are twelve men in
the gang and no room for all to sleep in the little shack. I'm a pitcher
with this outfit and get three dollars per day; if we go over to
Richardson's in a week, to thresh his stacks, I'll get $4 a day.
Another nasty effect of these cold days is the ease with which you
sprain your muscles while pitching.

LOG VALLEY, 3rd DECEMBER 1912

Everything is fine here also. Alas, the three-dollar-days are now finished, but there's still a dollar or so around for me to earn. The crops around here have all been threshed, and everybody was more than satisfied; nobody had dared to expect to much. Wheat ran about 28 to 32 bushels an acre and Jim Bedford's 40 acres produced 42 bushels per acre. This land had been worked more than that of my immediate neighbours. Even the grade of the wheat and flax is better than anyone had even expected; everything was between number one and two. It's too bad that the prices are so low, wheat was 58 cents a bushel in town last week and even flax was below the dollar. For a couple of days it was even as low as 75 cents. The price of flax see-saws amazingly, sometimes between today and tomorrow there's a difference of 5 cents per bushel. But the people need money to pay their notes. They have to sell at low prices because they can't wait until the New Year when the prices usually go up. So much wheat comes to Morse that the elevators can't handle it any more and a car shortage develops on the railroad.

You count yourself lucky if you can get rid of your wheat. This will probably get a lot worse in a couple of weeks. The river will be frozen then and all the men from across the river will arrive with their immense quantities of grain. Everybody here tries to get their wheat to town as quickly as possible in order to be ahead of the fellows from across the river. Steven is thinking of shipping his grain directly to Fort William in his own railroad car. I'll probably go to town for him on Thursday with a load of wheat. With my oxen I'll earn 15 cents per bushel; minus expenses I'll be left with 4 dollars. I'll see how the oxen bring it off and if they can do the work and everything goes well, then I can earn a day's wages once in a while, in that fashion. It is hard work, but in any case I wouldn't make more than 2 trips a week. I have to go to town anyway this week to buy a sleigh, so I can take a load of wheat along nicely. Last week I went to town for groceries and I asked about a sleigh. Well, they're pretty expensive, 40 dollars for the running gear alone, no box, neck-yoke, or doubletree; it's disappointing.

If I were to haul wheat this winter, I would also have to buy a box, as Janus is going to use his this winter to haul wheat to town.

That's another 20 dollars. You can't get a sleigh on time, but I fixed it with the implement agent that if I bought a plow, a disc, and a sleigh, I would get easier payment terms. I didn't go through with the deal right away because I thought I might send away to Eaton's for one. But there again you have to pay cash, and I have to keep a cent or two in my poke so I can buy another team of oxen this winter. So I plan to buy the whole outfit, and to sign the notes on Thursday. I'm buying $200 dollars' worth of implements; the first payment is in the fall of 1913, 80 dollars, the remainder in the fall of 1914.

I settled my accounts with Tom, and end this year with a surplus, in addition to the hay we still have for sale, I have 150 dollars for a team of oxen. I took out 30 dollars for provisions for this winter. If I can get some work with the oxen this winter, hauling wheat, hauling wood from the bush for one or another, I'll be able to clear that 80 dollars for provisions. Along with all that is the time that I've put in the breaking and building up of my land, which is now worth at least 6 dollars per acre.

HOME, 25th DECEMBER 1912

I went to town and bought a wagon, sleigh, and a plow for $213 and
I bought a team of oxen for 200 dollars. I didn't pay anything on
the implements as I got them on 2 payments, $63 on 1 November
1913 and $150 on 1 November 1914. I also didn't pay a cent for the
oxen yet. I have to pay $50 on the 1st of January, $25 on the 1st of
April 1913, and $125 on 1 November 1913. At present I possess 60
dollars, of which I owe $3 to K. for discing my land, $7.25 for 75
pounds of meat, and $4 for wood for a stable which I'm going to
build for the oxen. A part of the $40 will have to come out of the
hay; I expect my share to be worth about $30.

   That leaves 10 dollars which I hope to earn this winter by hauling
grain to town. I get 15 cents per bushel. To take a big load is the
way to do the job, but that all depends upon the condition of the
road. If the road is slippery, I wouldn't dare take a large load. It's
mostly the slipperiness which bothers the oxen. They'll pull 50
bushels to town as easily as 40, but if the road is slippery they aren't
worth very much. There are 5 elevators in town now, and it quite
often happens that they're all filled up and that they can't get any
cars to ship their grain in. Business then stands still for one, two, or
three days until they get rid of their grain. Streetbuyers, store-
keepers, and practically everybody who has a few spare dollars is
buying grain then, but of course they haven't got much storing room
and when they're filled up too, business comes to a standstill.
Farmers have to wait two or three days in town before they are able
to sell their loads. That's how it was last winter and that's how it's
going to be again this winter. So you see, hauling wheat to town is a
rather risky job for a fellow.

HOME, 1st JANUARY 1913

I bought 8 bushels of flax seed at $1.25 a bushel. It's Promost flax, an early variety; it ripens at least 10 days before other kinds of flax and so you avoid the chance of frost. I will still need about 12 bushels of wheat for seed, say 6 or 7 dollars, and at least $25 for provisions to last me until May. I've been busy lately hauling wood from the bush. Wood always comes in handy, what you don't burn this winter will burn twice as well this summer when it's dead and dry. There's an area in the bush where the fire went through last spring; the wood there is dry, cork dry. Naturally there is a lot of competition for this dry wood, but I managed to get 3 great big loads. It's almost finished now, but I found another place in the bush full of dry wood; I hope to be able to get another couple of loads from this area.

You ask me whether it pays to haul wood and burn it instead of coal. Well, I don't think so. Four or five loads of wood are equal to one ton of coal. Coal is just 8 dollars a ton in town, so a load of wood is only worth $2, and you have to saw it and split it and coal is simply easier to handle than wood. So you might say, in a way, it doesn't pay to burn wood, but just the same I am making $2 a day, and that's not too bad; I might contract with a fellow near town to fetch him 440 poplar fenceposts at 5 cents a piece, so a $22.00 job. I can fetch some 80 posts in a load, that's about 40 poles from 10 to 16 feet long. He wants posts 5 feet in length, so I cut 2 posts out of 1 pole.

LOG VALLEY, 9th JANUARY 1913

Suddenly winter arrived here. Friday, January 3, was still a beautiful day with only a few degrees of frost. Friday night the business began and Saturday it was 50 or 60 degrees below. The cold is constant, one day it might be a few degrees colder than the last; the daily averages are about 50 below. Sometimes it's so cold that my thermometer, which registers to 60 below, can't register the temperature because the liquid flows down into the little bulb.

Just as I thought, I got another job to haul grain to town. This week I took a load of 50 bushels to town; I got $7.50 for the job. I went with all 4 of my oxen. I hitched one team to the wagon and tied the other on the back, and after 10 miles (halfway to town) I gave them an hour's rest. I had dinner and after dinner I took the fresh team and tied the old one on the back of the wagon. I took all 4 along, not necessarily to pull, but because I didn't want to leave the oxen here for two whole days. I could leave them enough hay for a day or so, but what could I do about the water? And so I took the whole outfit along; the extra team raised my expenses by 50 cents, but they do make the job easier. I bought a three-horse-hitch in town for $4.50. I'm using this hitch on the wagon now and in the spring I'll also be able to use this hitch on my plow. I'll be able to run this outfit with three oxen in the event that one should get sick. So you can see, I got my money's worth.

If I go to town with a load of grain, I do it like this. I leave here early in the morning, better 6 than 7 o'clock. About 12 o'clock I reach the Lakes and I stop at Mr Hamm's. He's a German-Russian Mennonite who lives about 8 or 9 miles from my shack. I let my oxen drink the beautiful clear water, tie them to the wagon, and give them each an oat-sheaf. I earned 150 oatsheaves from Steven for hauling a load of wheat to town for him. Hamm gives me my dinner for 25 cents. I let the oxen rest for an hour or so, sometimes more, hitch them up again, and go as far as Mr Gregorius'. He's a German-American who lives 2 miles from town. Mr Gregorius is a contractor and lives on a farm which he acquired by homesteading. He's a well-to-do man and is friendly enough to let me stay overnight with my oxen. He has a beautiful stable which was just built this summer (it cost him 700 dollars on lumber alone) and a good comfortable house. It's a good place for me and my oxen to stay overnight. He wouldn't take money at first, but I made an agreement with him that I would give him a dollar a time in exchange for supper and breakfast, a good bed in his guest room, and a good supper and breakfast for my oxen.

Next morning I'm on the road again at 7, and about 8 I'm in town, just as the elevators are opening and Morse is waking up. Then it takes a little while before you get rid of the grain, if you have a lot of wagons ahead of you an hour or sometimes longer. Then I have my dinner in town, drive 6 or 7 miles, give my oxen a rest usually at sunset, and push on arriving home late in the evening. This week I arrived home at 9 o'clock; that's early because I used a fresh team on the way. It was also so bitterly cold that the oxen moved a lot faster than they are used to. It's hard hard work for the oxen and the driver, but you get real satisfaction out of it. After you put those few hard-earned dollars in your pocket, all that long road which you covered in the terribly bitter cold, and the unloading of the grain, seem worth it. Yes, you get that satisfaction, and the thankfulness and the sense of fulfillment. I bought $4 worth of groceries for my last load, 20 pounds of oatmeal, 20 pounds of sugar, 3 pounds of lard, 5 pounds of treacle, and 1 pound of baking powder.

HOME, 16th JANUARY 1913

I'm not planning to get rid of the oxen and buy horses in their place. Horses are more pleasant and accommodating and what not, but oxen do the same work. They are not as pleasant to work with, but they are cheaper, by a long shot. I think I'll go in for stock and cattle. The land around here is splendid for prairie grass, and I don't remember seeing anything like it in Canada. I won't invest my whole fortune in cattle; I'll also invest something in my farm. I'm going to buy good implements and build a good stable for my oxen. I'm also going to have a drill outfit dig me a good well, 40 or 50 feet deep, one that will give me a good water supply year round. I wouldn't hesitate to spend 100 dollars for a good well, and because I'm thinking of going in for cattle a good water supply is essential. And for a man who is going to have cattle, fencing is another essential; he doesn't want to chase after his cattle all over the prairie.

This fencing proposition takes a lot of money. I saw that this fall when I fenced 100 square yards of pasture for my oxen, just around the stable. I cut the posts in the bush, so they didn't cost me anything, just the labour, that's all. But the wire, the barbed wire, costs money! $3.50 a roll of 80 rods (440 yards). So one roll went around my pasture just once. I bought one roll and nailed it to the posts with staples, but naturally one roll isn't enough, I need another one. Two strings will do for oxen all right, but for cattle such as calves, you want 3 strings of wire. One roll is 80 rods, so you use 4 rolls per mile for a single string. That makes it 12 rolls per mile for 3 strings, that is, 42 dollars per mile. That's just the cost of the wire, without figuring in your time.

Because I'm planning to farm as well as graze cattle, I don't want to fence my own half section. Instead I'm thinking of renting section 11, the school section, from the government for grazing, and fencing that, either completely or in part. It's possible that I will also fence part of my land which is not as suitable for agriculture.

HOME, 24 JANUARY 1913

Unfortunately we are just about finished with our grain here, and I
don't know if it will be easy to haul wheat from across the river,
because you have to cross the ice with the oxen and they simply
refuse to do that. That reminds me of a nasty incident that occurred
during my last trip to town, one which gave me more trouble than I
had ever had before. The roads were very bad; we had some snow
and that made them very slippery. And slippery roads are the main
cause of trouble with oxen. They can't pull, of course, when they
haven't got a place to put their feet down.

I left Steven's along the Morse Trail, not the inside trail past my
shack, because the snow was more packed by the teams from across
the river and I didn't like to break my own trail along here. I never
drove this trail before, so the oxen didn't know it and neither did I. I
knew it, of course, I've been on it before, but never with a heavy
load on, and you might say you don't know a trail before you've
been on it with a load with oxen. You know every hill then and the
best way to get up. Of course the trail had been made by horses, all
horse teams, and I was the only ox team on the road, and a horse
will pull up a load easily where an ox cannot. *Not* because a horse is
stronger than an ox, but because an ox cannot travel on a slippery
road. If you go up a hill which is the least bit slippery, and if there is
a small hole in the road, say 6 to 12 inches deep, the oxen can't get
the load up. So I got stuck several times on the road, and I tell you
it's not very pleasant to get stuck halfway up a hill.

But anyway, somehow or another I pulled out every time, hitched
the oxen on the back of the wagon and pulled the load back down
the hill again. But all this takes lots of time and it plays out your
oxen as well as yourself. I had rather expected this and had left very
early that morning, long before daybreak. The moon was shining
bright, and when the sun finally rose I had put quite a few miles
behind me. Again, because I didn't want to have to break my own
trail, I stayed on the Morse Trail and I didn't go along to Hamm's
place, as I usually do.

At the Lakes, where I usually give my oxen a good rest, is a spring
with beautiful water which never freezes. Here I gave my oxen their
dinner, one oatsheaf each. When they had finished eating, I led them
to the water, but they refused to drink when the ice began to break

under them, and then the oxen and I broke through into the water. Luckily it was rather shallow there but I went up to my knees and I was wet, dripping wet, standing in that cold weather. For a second I was paralyzed with fear, but only a second, because the very next minute the oxen were hitched to the wagon and I was driving them as fast as they would go towards the closest shack, about a mile off. But just then we came to a bad hill and the hooves of the oxen were slippery from the frozen water. Quickly I scraped the ice off with my knife — it took me about 5 or 6 minutes — and then we were off again. Finally we reached the shack, as quick as the devil I thawed my shoes, pulled them off, and inspected my feet; my toes were just beginning to freeze.

I was wearing felt shoes and rubbers and it took me three hours to get them dry enough to wear so that there would be little danger of my feet freezing on the trail. So it was pretty late when I got to Gregorius' place, but just the same I made it, and made town and sold my wheat and came back again. The oxen are still tired from that trip. They're really some trips, but anyway you get home again and you soon forget your troubles. You get your stove going, and comfort yourself with a crackling fire in your own shack and the pleasure of a fine Dutch cigar.

HOME, 20 FEBRUARY 1913

We had some snow last week, lucky for the oxen too, they have to
eat snow because the well is not good enough to allow me to give
them water every day. I have delicious water in my well, but unfortunately not enough. The well was all right for a time; it gave a good
water supply in the spring of 1912, but in the summer and fall there
was less and less. That's the way it goes with most shallow wells
here, a good water supply for a little while and then they slowly dry
up. I can barely give my oxen water every other day and then not all
they want; whatever else they need they have to get by eating snow.
They're outside the whole day now, around my haystack, and they
never get very far away, always around the stable and the stack.
Eating snow is all right if there's enough snow and if it isn't too cold,
but it's not so pleasant if you're forced to put them out in bad
weather just to eat snow. I've brought snow into the stable for them
on cold windy days, but that's nothing more than half measure.
Once in a while I took them over to Steven's; he's lucky enough to
have a very good well.

There's a well outfit at my neighbour's now. A well-drilling
machine like that goes as deep as you want. If you dig a well yourself and reach water, you can go a foot or so deeper, but at a certain
point you have to quit. With a well-drilling machine you can go 40
or 50 feet deep, and you're practically certain to have 15 or 20 feet
of water the year round. That's a luxury, plenty of water, especially
if you have oxen; they can drink a tremendous amount of water.

I went to town with all 4 oxen. I hitched them in tandem to the
wagon, 2 to the shaft and 2 in front of them. It's a comical sight
with oxen, but it worked well, better than I had dared to expect. In
the beginning they had some trouble going downhill — if the front
team doesn't move ahead fast enough, the second team fouls their
traces with their feet — but later it went all right.

If I can, I'm going to buy registered Marquis wheat to sow my 8
acres, then I'll have enough Marquis seed grain the following year to
sow the new land I'm planning to break. This wheat will cost me 2
dollars per bushel, and because I'll need 12 bushels for 8 acres, it will
cost me 24 dollars. It truly isn't a small sum, but it's a beautiful investment. If I sow ordinary wheat — I can get it here for 50 cents a
bushel — it will cost me 6 dollars, but the extra 18 dollars will give
me a 100% interest. This Marquis wheat is pure, true to type, and it
won first prize in New York. And if I have more than I need for seed
after threshing, then I can always get a good price for it as seed
around here.

You shouldn't pamper yourself on the trail, it makes your skin
soft; it's better to be a little less comfortably rested out and to keep
your skin hard. Also as far as shoes are concerned, some people wear
3 or more pairs of socks and they keep their feet nice and warm, but
if the following day they put on only 2 pair instead of 3 they freeze
their feet. Keep your feet neither warm nor cold, and make certain
that your feet never sweat. That's the secret: toughen your body and
get acclimatized to the cold. Prevent sweating in the winter! Too
warm footwear makes the feet sweat, soaks shoes, and allows
freezing and rubbing.

Water in a good well is quite a thing here; at a good depth you
also get better water. The water in Canada has an injurious effect on
your teeth, and that's the reason that so many people in America
suffer from bad teeth. I've had trouble this winter too, two molars
and 2 front teeth have cavities. But to have them pulled or filled
costs a lot in Canada; these dentists are expensive rogues.

HOME, 13th MARCH 1913

We thought last week that spring was arriving; it thawed practically the whole week, the snow disappeared quickly and put the roads in bad condition. Once the snow starts to melt, you realize that there was more on the ground than you thought. I made my last trip to town on the 6th and 7th of March. The roads were thoroughly bad, but you'll get there with the 'four.' It's been freezing again since the day before yesterday and the weather is getting generally colder again, 30 degrees of frost, 2 fahrenheit degrees above zero. I hauled another load for R., flax this time because I've already taken all his wheat to town. Thank to the nourishing feed I give the oxen, they withstood the trips very well.

I still don't have any seed wheat, and I'm afraid that I won't be able to afford to buy from a seed firm; I hope to buy pure Red Fife from someone close to town for a dollar a bushel, an expenditure of 12 dollars; this money will have to come out of the hay. We already sold a load of hay for 5 dollars and I'm sure the man will need more as soon as the men can cross the river again with their wheat. This isn't safe at the present time because of last week's thaw. So I'm hoping for some more cold winter weather. If the river is safe to cross again, then S. will get people stopping and he'll need hay. He'll have to come to us because Janus and I have the monopoly on hay. We offered him the two stacks we had for sale for 70 dollars. He was quite interested as part of the sale price could be paid 'on time.' He could give each of us a pregnant sow, 20 or 25 dollars each, and the rest in cash in the fall. But I would rather see some money.

LOG VALLEY, 23 MARCH 1913

The oxen are in good shape. They get good food and they look in
top form despite all the work they've done this winter. They look
better than most oxen around here which earned nothing this
winter, and ate into last harvest's hard-earned money. We hoped that
spring was practically here but Jack Frost played a dirty trick on us.
Forster, the weather prophet, had forecast in his bulletin in the *Free
Press*, 'keep a weather-eye open during the 16-28th of March period,'
and believe it or not it began exactly on the 16th of March. It was
snowing Monday morning, but the weather did look a bit better.
That morning I was ready at 5 o'clock to hitch up, and I thought I
would take a chance. While I was under way it got worse and worse
and by 9 o'clock it was a complete blizzard.

In some places I couldn't see a sign of the road, and behind me
the wagon left no trail because the wind quickly filled it with snow
and wiped it out. But never mind, the oxen and I know the road, we
know every hill and every curve; I wasn't afraid. Around 10 o'clock
it was at its worst, we drifted off the road and plodded through the
deep snow until after 20 minutes (they seemed like 20 hours) we
reached the road again. I was planning to stop at the first shack and
wait till next day but all at once it cleared up. The wind, which had
blown from all directions before, steadied from the North-West, the
snow slowly stopped, it got a little warmer, and in the afternoon the
weather was all right. A romantic tale, but blizzards are mischievous
rascals.

In the winter or in the fall, you can easily get oxen with a small
cash payment, but naturally not in the spring. *One* horse costs
money, but with *two horses* you *make* money. Janus took some
wheat into town, for Mr. P., in the beginning of the winter. He took
6 or 7 loads and received 2½ dollars a trip; you don't make any
money that way, only enough for a pair of shoes and some tobacco.
Janus has become the resident agent in Log Valley for the 'Netherlands Mortgage Company.' He can probably earn some money that
way this summer, however, I think he's being just a little bit opti-
mistic. If a homesteader fulfills his duties for 3 years and has received his patent (deed) the Mortgage company will lend him money
on his land. They give him a mortgage, usually for 1000 dollars. This

money is to be returned in payments within 5 years at 7, or in some companies, at 8%. Janus' company lends money at 8%, he gets 1% commission, so 10 dollars for a loan of 1000 dollars.

HOME, 29th APRIL 1913

I sold my oxen to my neighbour for 400 dollars, 125 cash and the rest in the fall of this year. We had warm weather for 3 weeks right after the spring thaw, and I saw how little you can count on oxen in warm weather. At first I worked them very slowly for short periods in order to get them used to the work and the warmth. But even after a long time they blew like machines; then I decided to sell them if I could get a good price for them, and enough cash for a down payment of 4 horses. You can figure to break 2 acres a day with 4 horses but you're not sure of even one with oxen. It all depends on the weather. This, especially, decided me to sell them.

I'm planning to get 100 acres broken this summer, and because the breaking season is so short, 10 May to 1 July, a person has to make good headway. You can break until the middle of August or September in a wet year, but land that's broken that late just doesn't produce the crop that earlier broken land does. Furthermore there's another problem; I have to break those 100 acres myself because no-one here is willing to break for anyone else during breaking time. They'll do it after July but not before they have used the best time for themselves. And no wonder, if you see the difference between early and late breaking.

Horses are expensive; a 4-horse team costs 900 dollars or more and 4 oxen 400 dollars. But when you realize, weather permitting, that you can have 100 acres broken by the 1st of August with horses, and that this early breaking is worth 5 dollars per acre as contrasted to 4 for later breaking, so 500 dollars value, and that oxen can only break about 50 acres in the same time, then the difference in price is considerably smaller. And added to this is the fact that you can make more money with horses in late summer, harvest, and wintertime than you can with oxen in cultivating, threshing, or wheat hauling. Opposed to this is the fact that horses cost more to feed than oxen. A horse cannot work without oats, and an ox can if it must. Four horses eat about 10 bushels of oats a week, so 3 dollars per week. Three dollars worth of oats will last 4 oxen a month. But this extra food for the horses produces much more work.

I haven't bought any horses yet. I saw some horses in town which were for sale, but I'm a little wary of them. A fellow doesn't sell a horse in this country if it's any good at all; he keeps it. Well, I saw

some good horses in town, but most of them have just been shipped
in from the Station or from down East (Ontario-New York), and a
man certainly runs a risk buying one of those horses; they aren't
used to the climate out here and a lot of them die the first winter.
Another thing about P.'s horses, they've been born on the ranch, are
used to the climate, are out all winter, and they're tough. A man
might have a bit of trouble breaking them at first, but treat them
gently, never abuse them, and take good care of them, and they are
sure to make good horses. I believe a man is a lot smarter to buy a
horse from a rancher than to buy a horse from somebody else. As
a rule, a horse that's had too many different drivers isn't much any-
more. An investment in horses is a good investment; horses are just
as good as money. As far as ready cash is concerned I'm all right.

Janus has begun to break with his 2 horses and a walking plow, a
12-inch plow. Handling a walking plow is quite a trick and it takes a
man quite a while to get into it. W. wrote me that he would advise
me not to plant Marquis wheat on new breaking. He says that
Marquis needs loose soil and only then do you get a good sample. I
now have beautiful oats for seed. I cleaned them very carefully, and,
weather permitting, they ought to give me a good crop. If you have
horses it's well worth your while to have your own oats. You lose an
awful lot of time hauling wheat to town and hauling oats back. I
borrowed a farming mill and cleaned the oats through and through; I
sieved out more than 10 bushels so that only the largest grains
remained for seed.

I bought some radish seed in town and I'd like to sow some more
vegetables, but I'm afraid of what the gophers will do. Radishes are
the only things they don't eat.

The first place where a newcomer goes to work is a very im-
portant influence. Had I started with a man like Jack Webb, I would
have immediately formed a trust in this country, but at E.'s and
Burrill's, life was miserable, wretched enough to discourage the most
courageous.

HOME, 4 MAY 1913

I bought a team of sorrel horses from the Big Coulee Ranch, good
sturdy horses, weighing about 1400 pounds apiece. I brought them
home Friday afternoon, a real job, as they are broncos. First we
hitched them to the harrow and then to the plow. They went all
right once they were hitched up, but it's a big job to hitch them.
You take your life in your hands because the smallest thing will turn
them into frenzied kickers. I don't trust them, they're too quick and
turn too quickly. They might be all right after a while, but for the
first month or so you need another fellow to help you hitch them.
That means quite a bit, as we aren't overcrowded with neighbours
here yet, and everyone has his own business to look after. I bought
those horses for 450 dollars, payable November 1st. They're worth
the money all right because they're big horses. But I should have
bought those broncos a month sooner, and should have had them in
the stable for a while to give them a chance to get used to being
handled by a man. They would have been all right by now, but they
are scared and nervous and they hardly eat the food I give them.
They haven't had a drink since I got them. They must feel pretty dry
by now, but they won't drink.

HOME, 9 MAY 1913

It was quite a job to get the mail this time! It began on Thursday, 2nd of May, a sudden 'change in the weather,' rain, hail, wind, and cold. Janus came home on Friday; the boss had realized that there wasn't going to be much work done for a couple of days. Friday was much the same, rain again and hail and towards the evening it began to snow. It fell steadily the whole night and by Saturday the ground was well covered. Slowly but surely it became a full-blown blizzard, the snow whipped across the prairie and visibility was less than a 100 yards.

There was no chance to go and get the mail in the afternoon, no matter how much we wanted to. Still we sat around convincing each other that it really wasn't that bad and we should at least give it a try. Finally we got as far as drawing lots, to see which one would go. The choice fell on me. So I pulled on my winter boots, took my sheepskin and winter cap out of the trunk — I had put them away hoping they would stay there until next winter — and set out with the dogs hoping they would help me find the road. I had gone about a half a mile, when I realized the absolute impossibility of the trip, and no matter how much it goes against a fellow's principles to turn back, I turned back and found my way back to the shack. Most of *my* footprints were swept away, but I found the way back by the dog tracks, as these were much deeper in the snow than mine.

Sunday morning came, and Sunday afternoon, but there was very little change. We still came to the conclusion, as we had the day before, that someone had to go. As a sidelight was the materialistic consideration that 'we were out of grub,' and Steven has pork and eggs for sale. During the period from Thursday or Friday we had lived on bread and beans, and after being on a diet like that for a couple of days a fellow begins to feel a little peckish, and gets a real desire for a less vegetarian meal. Anyway Janus said, 'I'll give it a try, maybe I'm luckier than you were yesterday.' I tried to dissuade him but as he already had his shoes on, I thought he might as well see how his chances were. Now the weather was so grim again, and the blowing snow whipped your face so terribly, that a trip like that looked more like a desperate deed than anything else.

In any case I expected Janus back within an hour or so, or if the weather did clear up he would probably make it as far as Steven's.

But I didn't think he would find the road from Steven's to Walter's, and if he did, he would probably get lost. Strange, but that's exactly what happened. When he had been gone for about a half hour it cleared up a bit, it got a little lighter, but it was raw weather and stayed that way. I waited and waited, every five minutes I looked out, but no Janus in sight; darkness began to fall very quickly, it was 7:30. Just as I was considering what measures to take now, I saw one of the dogs approaching, and a couple of minutes later Janus and Fannie appeared out of the haze. 'Well, what have you got?' 'Eggs,' says Janus with a great broad smile, 'no mail, lost my way between Steven's and Walter's.'

Well, Monday morning came but not much of an improvement. In the afternoon, about one o'clock, it cleared up more and more, it got a lot brighter, so that you could see about a quarter of a mile. I went to Steven's and then to Walter's to get the mail. 'Fine day,' Walter says, 'just the kind of weather a fellow living in a sodhouse is looking for. Just look on the floor, what a mess it's made of this here post office!' The whole floor was inundated, the water took no notice of us and just continued dripping steadily.

Tuesday the weather changed, the snow slowly melted away in the morning, the melting speeded up in the afternoon, and by evening very little was left. In the afternoon we went to George's; I asked him if I could borrow his pony on Wednesday to go to town. 'Well,' George says, 'you might just as well go to town on her back, cause that cart ain't too strong and Charlie's buggy's gone all together, just collapsed, that's all there is to it. I've fixed that there cart of mine, you know, the spring is broken, and so I just fixed it with a piece of rope, of course it might hold, but just as likely it might not; it's a kind of risky job anyhow, and if you take the cart, you'd better take a couple of spare ropes with you in case you get a breakdown on the way.'

The axle was simply tied to the seat with a rope. Two wheels joined by a long axle to prevent tipping, the spring on top of that, the seat on top of the spring joined to the axle by a length of rope. If the rope breaks you lose the wheels, a rather unpleasant surprise at any time.

I arrived at George's early Wednesday morning at about 6 o'clock. George asked me to go to Morse along the Ernfold route so that I could pick up the spring, that he had ordered a couple of weeks ago,

to fix up his rig. Ernfold is 16 miles south-east, while Morse is dead
south. Ernfold is closer to us than Morse, but because there isn't an
actual road from there to here, we always go to Morse. 'Well, Bill,'
George says, 'I guess I'd better tell you the road then, as far as I can
that is to say, there ain't no road at all, but I'll tell you the easiest
way to get there. Now listen, you first go 2 miles east, then dead
South, for, well, I don't know how long, but you'll see a big hill,
then you go around that hill Westward, till you cross the Swift Current Trail — there used to be a trail last fall — just follow that for
awhile, then turn to your left again, and then — well, Bill, I'm sure
you will find it, it's easy enough, and you'll see a firebreak to the
East, somewhere around 8 miles from here; you can follow that for a
couple of miles, if you like, but one thing, Bill, don't go too far East;
it's just 8 miles between Ernfold and Morse, so you'll know the
direction a bit.'

Naturally with those directions I couldn't miss it! The most unbelieveable thing is that we reached Ernfold. The village itself lay
tucked away behind a high hill, and it was quite a surprise, to Polly
and myself, to suddenly see the elevators and houses only a half mile
from us. The cart had held up quite well till now. It had undergone
quite an ordeal because there are quite a few stones and a lot of
badger holes on the prairie, but we arrived at Ernfold without acci-
dent. I put Polly in the livery barn, went to the implement man to
ask for the new spring, which unfortunately had not arrived. At
about 11 I went to the Chinaman's to eat some dinner; all that
shaking and bumping over the stones had made me hungry. I stayed
in Ernfold till 12:30. Just follow the railroad track, and I did. That's
all right in flat country, but it was pretty hilly here and there and we
had to go around the hills and then back along the track again. We
had probably gone 4 miles westward like that when suddenly Polly
took to her heels and ran across the flat as if she were possessed.
Something must have scared her because she was completely stam-
peded. I had enough trouble just trying to control Polly to turn
around to see what had scared her. Then without warning a train
raced by. I hadn't heard the train coming up behind us because of
the strong wind. The train was already far in the distance, but Polly
ran on; the fright had probably gone to her legs. We arrived in Morse
but received another disappointment. My suit, the cause for the
whole trip, couldn't be found. I let Polly rest for a couple of hours

in the livery barn, so that she would recover from her fright. We left
Morse at 4:30 and arrived home at 7 o'clock. It was quite a trip for
Polly, 50 miles (80 km), but she's used to it, as is every horse here.
This afternoon the rain began, rain and hail; tonight it's pouring and
awfully dark.

HOME, 19 MAY 1913

I bought 2 horses, both geldings, weighing about 1300 and 1400 pounds, two big strong horses. I bought them for 550 dollars, 50 dollars cash and 500 dollars on time. I'm pretty busy these days picking stones, and I tell you that there are quite a few once you start picking them. It's a very satisfying job, every stone you've picked and piled up won't bother you again.

HOME, 12 JUNE 1913

Breaking is such heavy work at present that my neighbours have temporarily abandoned it, but my horses pull the plow as if it were no weight at all. I could probably go on with my breaking if it wasn't for the fact that you can do a better job of plowing after some rain. I've made an agreement with one of my neighbours to disc for him now, and later on, after some rain, he will break for me. He has oxen and they're too slow for discing. For every 4 acres I disc, he'll break one. I think I'll probably be able to disc 8 or 9 acres a day with my outfit, so that earns about 2 acres of breaking. An acre of breaking is worth 4 dollars, so I can earn about 8 dollars a day. What a pleasure to have horses now instead of oxen. No yelling all day long: get on, come on, get up now, move on boys; the horses go by themselves, and instead of having to urge them to work, I have to continually hold them back. Farming is a lot easier now.

I now regularly have 15 foot of water, 40 feet down, in my well. That's more than enough for a well with a 2-foot diameter. The well is so good that it's practically too good. I didn't have enough cattle to water to keep the water fresh, and now and then I had to empty it. But now that I have 4 horses and water them 3 times a day, I use a lot of water and it stays fresh. I hired a hand for picking stones at a dollar-fifty a day.

HOME, 22 JUNE 1913

Breaking is a little easier after a rain, but it's still too dry. The crop on the spring breaking will probably be a failure this year. A lot of the flax and oats on spring breaking was sown too late, and very little of it has germinated because of the lack of rain the last 2 weeks. And a crop of spring breaking, especially flax, needs rain right after seeding. I make an average of 7 or 8 dollars a day with my horses. Tomorrow I'm going to work on the road for the municipality and I'll get 7 dollars a day. This goes toward the reduction of my taxes; my assessment is 10 dollars per quarter section. In May we had beautiful weather for oxen, it was cooler than usual and we had a lot of rain; this makes breaking very easy. A. broke 35 acres, but now he's fed up with driving oxen, he hates it, and he says it's too hard on them. The mosquitoes bother them all day long, and then once in a while the gadflies go after them.

Gadflies are a strange cattle pest; they don't seem to bother horses at all, just cattle. The gadfly is a sort of wasp; it aims at the heels of the cattle and so it is also called a heel-fly. Cattle simply become frantic when the gadflies go after them, and nothing can hold them. Some days there are hundreds, and other days you don't see any.

HOME, 30 JUNE 1913

I'll take the opportunity now to tell you what all we have been
doing this week. Rain, rain, and more rain, good for the crops and
good for breaking. I'd say we had 7 days of rain and so we couldn't
do much breaking, just a little between the storms, but not a full
day's work. We'll probably make up our lost time this week, the
breaking is a lot easier now that the sod is thoroughly wet. I think
we'll have good breaking for ten days or so, and in those ten days I
hope to break another 20 acres or so. I've now broken a good 20
acres, and Andrew Graham owes me another 4 acres for the discing I
did for him. The horses are working fine, and I've got enough power.
The horses and I can get a good day's work in, be tired at night, but
never too tired, and after a night's rest we're fresh again in the morning, ready to start work anew. I plowed an acre this morning, but my
shear was so dull that it wouldn't cut very well. It was my last shear,
as all my other shears were dull, and I had given them to Rooker last
night to have them sharpened in town. I can't plow till he comes
back tomorrow night, but never mind, I can find lots of other work.

This afternoon I've been picking stones, picking them up with the
wagon and piling them up in one great heap. Tomorrow I'll be at the
same job; I hope I'll be through by tomorrow night, and have the
other 20 acres cleared. I'm now plowing on the west side of my land,
along the mile side. I make eight rounds a day, that's a day's work,
and if the weather is all right, I'll do it every day. Eight rounds with
a 14-inch shear is just a little bit more than 2 acres.

LOG VALLEY, 13 OCTOBER 1913

When it began to rain Saturday afternoon, and Steven and I couldn't
work, I decided to walk to Morse to find Mate. I left here at 2
o'clock in the afternoon, kept up a good pace, and reached town at
7:30. It had been pitch dark since 7, but I knew the road all too
well, and besides that I walked towards the railroad lights. The stores
were still open, in honour of Saturday night and harvest time, and so
I was still able to buy a pair of overalls and a pair of gloves, and to
get a haircut. That night I slept well in a Chinese restaurant. I
should have told you, they had a big fire in Morse not so long ago;
the hotel, a couple of stores, and 2 livery barns went up in flames. It
was a wonder that the whole town didn't burn down, because when
you get a fire in a town composed of nothing but wooden buildings,
then usually the whole business burns up. That fire certainly
changed Morse in a very short time; it's twice as big now as it was
last winter. Now there are 5 elevators, 2 hotels under construction,
livery barns, lumberyards, I don't know how many more businesses.
Early Sunday morning I left to find Mate, and I was lucky enough to
find her at a farmer's, exactly where I hoped she would be. We were
very happy, Mate and I, to have found each other again. The day I
lost her, she must have been confused; she followed the farmer home
and stayed there. It was difficult for him to give her up, but he said
he was very pleased that she had found her master again.
    Sunday afternoon I reached my shack again. Quickly I went to
take a look at Janus' shack, and unfortunately, just as I had expected, the whole north side had caved in. That's too bad! This week we
got more rain and snow, and so we couldn't work for a couple of
days. So I dug a cellar for Steven and earned 1½ dollars a day. I
wasn't as lucky this week as last, when I worked 5½ days at 3 dollars
a day, so altogether 16½ dollars. It's now Sunday evening, it's a
beautiful night and tomorrow promises to be another nice day. I
hope to wangle a few dollars this week, if the weather stays good.
When I had been home for only an hour this afternoon, Janus turned
up to get the mail I was keeping for him in my shack.
    The threshing outfit is now 2 miles east of us. First they'll go
further north, and only then will they come here to thresh our settlement. The outfit doesn't work particularly well and is slow, so we
all put our heads together, and now Steven and Tom plan to buy a

small 15-horsepower threshing outfit. They hope to have the outfit here in about 10 days. It's quite an undertaking, but I think they'll make it.

Four hundred dollars, you can really do something with that here! Janus is planning to buy a couple of horses, and then haul wheat into town this winter. He also wants to buy 2 more horses this spring and some young cattle. With 400 dollars he's a long way there already. I hope you understand that he's buying everything 'on time.' That's the accepted way to purchase things here. If you can put 250 dollars down on a 4-horse team, you're all right. He'll surely give up his pension now that he sees his future laid out before him. You're probably wondering how 400 dollars could be his future, but it is true.

LOG VALLEY, 28 OCTOBER 1913

Steven and Tom have bought a threshing outfit; it's their only chance of getting their threshing done. It's a Case outfit, costing $2800, to be paid in 4 annual instalments of $700. There's 600 acres to be threshed here, so a good ten days. Janus is still working for the E. outfit with the oxen, he earns $6 per day, of which I get $2 for the use of my oxen. He keeps $4 for his wages and rental of his wagon and hay rack. I make $3 per day at Steven's, so I make $5 altogether. That's a beautiful wage, I wish it could last for another month; unfortunately it's finished much too soon. Generally the middle of November is 'freeze-up' and the ground doesn't unthaw until spring.

We have snapdragons in three colours, white, yellow, and purple. Around here they call the flower loco-weed, especially the purple one because the purple loco-weed causes a sickness in horses. Once a horse acquires the taste, he becomes crazy about it and is lost. He is, as they say 'locoed.' He becomes blind and walks around in a daze, he becomes crazy and it's impossible to cure him. The ranchers have had a lot of trouble with it. G.S., the one that had the post office, has it among his horses; 3 died last week and 2 yesterday, all colts. The horses that have it usually don't die, they just go crazy.

Janus bought a horse for 125 dollars. It's a nice horse, 2½ years old, buckskin colour, sturdily built. The horse isn't broken yet, a bronc, an animal that, up to now, has spent its whole life on the open free prairie. How is this horse to be trained? Janus left it tied to the wagon rack for a day, but it kicked it completely apart. Then he built a fence next to his shack with a length of barbed wire he had found on the way home. He put the horse inside the fence, and tied him to a pole which he drove two feet into the ground. Next morning we found the horse inside the fence but he had pulled the pole out of the ground. It was a wonder he was still inside the fence because, if he had wanted, he could have gotten out very easily. When I went to look this morning to see if the horse was still there, the bird had flown the coop. We searched the whole district but didn't find him. He had a rope around his neck, and on that a pole, so he probably won't get very far in such a short time. He can walk but he can't run.

We had bad weather this week for threshing and in addition the separator had a breakdown. So we haven't done anything this week. What have I done then? Well, I harrowed those 8 acres again with the oxen, did a little work for Steven, and yesterday I went to the bush for a load of firewood. I managed to gather a good pile of dry, dead wood, it burns as if for the fun of it.

P.S. After a whole day's search we finally found the horse.

HOME, 28th OCTOBER 1913

I've been hauling up my water out of the well by way of a pail and rope, a tiresome and time-consuming job, so I sent down to Eaton's for a pump. I put it in yesterday, tried it, and it wouldn't work. I tried it again this morning, poured in some hot water first, and it went fine. The pump and the piping and the freight from Winnipeg cost me close to 20 dollars, but I believe it's a sure-paying investment, and in the winter it's too cold to haul up water with a pail.

While I'm writing about the well I might as well give you exact information as to its construction. The hole in the ground is 40 ft deep, 2 feet in diameter and round. I've got it lined with 2-inch lumber, boards straight up and down, 2 boards, 6-inches wide to the round, so that the diameter of the well after curbing is about 20 inches. About 3 feet of the curbing sticks out about the well. It's a wonderful blessing, a good well. My neighbours often come to visit with their oxen. Now I'm not opposed to that, because there's always enough water, as long as they make sure that the oxen don't come to the well on their own and start wandering around my hay and oatsheaves. But they can't always control their oxen and once in while one whips over here to have a good drink. I've now fenced my oats and hay and the rascals can't get at them.

G.'s horses broke loose once in a while and on the way they would do some damage to my stooks. The best thing to do is to take them to the pound and charge damages. Our district poundkeeper lives about 5 miles South-East. If you find cattle on your land you can take them there, and the owner can claim his cattle after he had paid the damages you ask. But you don't like to do that to a neighbour, and all you do is warn him to keep an eye on his stock in the future. One of G.'s horses ate too much wheat and died here, right on the trail about a hundred yards North of my stack. I told him to move it out of the road, but he doesn't seem willing to do so. I don't want that dead horse in front of my shack. The horses become skittish when you drive them by, and besides, the wolves are tiresome, howling around the house at night, and sometimes waking me up. The horses are all fine and dandy, and in the prime of condition, they all have their winter coats already, and I don't think I'll have any trouble bringing them through the winter. I give them plenty of exercise, keep them out of the stable all day, and I make them exercise.

LOG VALLEY, 15th NOVEMBER 1913

I had 4 oxen, I was planning to keep my oxen and stick the money into cattle. I wasn't planning to put everything in ranching, part of it was to be an investment in farming, but only as much as was absolutely necessary. Through my trips to town with wheat I made the acquaintance of Mr G. Last summer he had 6 horses, 4 big ones and 2 smaller. He worker with the 4 big horses and had the lighter team (they weighed about 1100 lbs apiece, I guess) as a reserve for light farmwork, cutting hay, harrowing, etc. In late summer 2 of his big horses died, and when I met him last winter he had 2 big horses and 2 smaller ones, so not a matched 4-horse team. He was planning to sell the lighter team and buy a big team in their place to work with his own big team. After I received your letter I began to think how it would be if I bought that team from him. I could hire a man to work my oxen, and I would work the small team myself, working up the land, discing with a small disc, and harrowing. Later in the summer I could go to the bush with them and haul wood for fence poles. Later on I could make hay; hay was especially desirable because I would need quite a bit of it for my cattle. I could find plenty to do for the team, while the hired hand worked the oxen, so there was profit on both sides.

I made an agreement with G. that I would buy the team in the spring for 400 dollars, and I would pay him that summer. I didn't take the team in the winter because I had no stable room, work, or feed. That's the way things stood this spring. Then early this spring I began to disc and harrow the 8 acres again; for the first time I used oxen on the disc. They moved awfully slow and blew, like I don't know what, but it went all right. Then I saw a way to make more money. I had already bought 2 horses; if I traded these oxen in towards a 2nd team, then I would have 4 horses, they would cost more on feed, but they would also break twice as much land and right in the breaking season of May and June. It was only a thought yet, and I hadn't given it my full consideration when A. and S. arrived looking for 4 oxen to buy. They came to my place, we started dealing and reached an agreement. I sold the oxen on good conditions, I got 125 dollars cash, a note on the balance, and I wasn't worried as to the payment of the balance because I knew that S. had sold his westerly homestead and that he would receive 300 dollars in the fall. Besides that it was a good down payment, which would allow me to make a cash payment on the 2nd team of horses and to buy feed. So I sold my oxen and did the dumbest thing I've ever done in my whole life, and now I'm suffering the consequences. Then G. told me he'd rather not sell me his team, putting me in a nasty situation, as I now had to buy 4 big horses with a big cash payment. G. offered his 4 horses for 1050 dollars, 75 dollars cash and the rest in the summer. He didn't want to sell only his light team, but the whole outfit. I didn't feel much like it, but I didn't want to break off negotiations, as he knew and trusted me. I offered him 1000 dollars but he didn't accept it. Hindsight says that I was stupid that I didn't buy the team on his conditions. Selling the oxen was my first mistake, not buying G.'s 4 horses for 1050 was my second mistake.

Then I went to town; I saw several horses for sale in the livery stable, but as I was unknown it was high prices and big cash payments, and for poor horses. Then I saw 12 horses, 3 four-horse teams. I chose 4 and in the evening I saw the owner, asked his prices and made an agreement to buy 2 teams, my black team for 550 dollars and the other one for 600 dollars, 75 dollars cash and the rest in the summer. He would also sell me the necessary harness on time. The next day we went to his farm to get the horses. Then he told me that the sale of the horses on time, with 75 dollars cash, was all right, but that he wanted cash for the harness and that he didn't want to sell it on time. So I was stuck, horses without harness were not much good to me, and I didn't have enough money to buy harnesses.

We saw some other horses and in the evening we saw the owner in town. He said he would sell me a team for a 50-dollar cash payment, and because I had seen a second-hand harness that evening at the saddler's for 25 dollars, I decided, after long consideration, to buy his black team for 550 dollars. So 50 dollars cash and 25 dollars for the saddler's gave me a team and harness for 75 dollars. I couldn't buy another team so I went home with 2 horses. You can't do any farmwork with 2 horses. You can always find work to do such as picking stones, but it was such beautiful weather for breaking, that every evening you felt like pulling the hair out of your head in frustration. And that was after you had worked the whole day long, doing the only work you could do with 2 horses. If I had bought G.'s team I could have gone directly to work and probably have

broken 50 acres more than I have now, especially as I would be
breaking in the right season. So you can see why I should have
bought G.'s horses; even if I would have had to pay him 50 dollars
more than I offered, it would have paid me.

Once in a while I would go into town to try and buy a second
team, till finally I bought a team of mares with harness for 600
dollars. They were 50 dollars too expensive, but with everything on
time, I would soon earn that 50 dollars by getting directly to my
breaking. But just as I got going fairly well, it got too dry. I'm going
to go on plowing, but breaking in dry weather makes the land very
difficult to disc, and besides that it doesn't rot and it won't produce
as good a crop next year as good breaking. What shall I ascribe it
to? Not only bad luck, but in large part it's my own fault for making
such big mistakes.

Expense Account

Oatsheaves	20.00
Interest on team of geldings	10.00
Interest on team of mares	4.75
Groceries and meat	100.00
Hardware (machine-oil, grease, bolts, etc.)	5.00
Blacksmith	12.00
Threshed oats	30.00
Eggs and butter	6.00
I don't figure wages, as wages are an improvement on my land, it's worth a dollar an acre to get the stones off.	
Baking flour into bread	6.00
For pork and coal so far as used	2.00
For feeding my own oatsheaves, I'm figuring my crop of oats as worth 125 dollars, of which I've already fed 45 dollars, will feed 40 this winter, and will have 45 dollars' worth left this spring	45.00
Depreciation of implements	60.00
Feed for horses from now till spring (4 months)	40.00
Own living expenses during winter and coal, 50 dollars of which I should earn, 25 dollars as my wages for looking after horses this winter	25.00
	365.75

And now the work I've done with my horses. I'll figure it up in dollars, because if someone else had to do the work, I would have to pay him so much.

40 acres breaking	160.00
40 acres double discing	80.00
40 acres double harrowing	20.00
For Graham and Sweeting	75.00
10 acres late (fall) breaking	40.00
8 acres stubble plowing (my oatfield)	20.00
8 acres double-discing (same)	8.00
Work done	403.00
Expenses	365.75
	37.25

Roadwork for municipality of Vermilion Hills	7.00
Cutting my oats at 75 cents an acre	6.00
	13.00

Cash on team of geldings 50.00
One set of secondhand harness 25.00
Oatsheaves from H. and R. 20.00
Note on team of mares and set of harness at
   8% interest 604.75
Note of team of geldings and interest at 10% 510.00
Note on oxen and interest at 10% for 7 months 158.75
(Later on I made an agreement with the fellow from
   whom I bought the oxen that I would pay him 150
   dollars in the summer, instead of 25 dollars in the
   spring and 125 dollars in the fall. I had the money
   to pay him in the spring, but preferred to keep this
   money in hand.)
R.H.Mc —. for well-drilling and interest 56.25
(He first dug a well 15 feet deep and struck sand and
   water; I would have had a good supply of water there but
   it was always liable to be sanded up and would have to be
   cleaned up every once in a while. So I told him to try
   another place, where we struck water at a depth of 40 ft.
   But I had to pay him for that 15-ft well just the same.)

Lumber for stable and interest at 8%	193.55
Note on implements and interest	109.00
Eaton's order (underwear, shirts, halters for the horses, 2 common chairs, a couple of overalls, wire stretchers, shoes, camera, films, paint for stable, rivets, snaps, wrenches, a suit of clothes and a new hat to go to church with, etc., and freight and bed and mattress)	64.85
Lumber for well curbing	25.00
Groceries and meat since spring (rather much as I had somebody working with me for a while)	100.00
Hardware, nails, track for barn doors, taps, pails, coaloil, bolts, axle-grease, machine oil, hinges, windows, tarpaper for stable, bindertwine (I used 20 pounds for my 8 acres of oats, costs me 14 cents a pound; a very handy article around the place, you fix a lot of things with bindertwine and barbed wire). A farmer at Indian Head had an automobile which he repaired in several places with those ingredients.	30.00
Groom fees for the mares. I've got to pay 10 dollars apiece for getting my mares served if they are both in foal, of which I'm not quite sure yet. I made 3 special trips to town to get them served, so by rights I should deserve to get two nice colts out of them.	6.00
Total expenses	1953.15
Blacksmith, sharpening of shears, shoeing my horses and some repairs	12.00
Threshed oats and bags	32.00
Eggs and butter, Hamm on the Lakes	6.00
Mrs Street for baking 2 bags of flour into bread	6.00
Wages picking stones and stacking, etc.	55.00
Dog	5.00
Pump from Eaton's, piping, rods, and freight	19.50
Eaton's order, a good warm fur coat (dogskin), 20 dollars' worth of winter shoes and socks, a new bucksaw, mitts, a pair of blankets, a pair of Mackinaw pants, bolts, etc., and freight	42.75
Note for 4 breaking shears	16.00
30 pounds of fresh pork	6.00

Subscription to papers	4.00
Two rolls of barbed wire and staples (to finish my fence and for a fence around my stacks)	7.50
2300 pounds of coal, of which I have already used 300	9.20
	2174.10

This is a very general list of my expenses, far from complete. The list goes on with different expenses such as stamps, picture-business, running to town (which is rather expensive; I made trips to get the mares served), for the sharpening of shears, for groceries, etc., close to a total of 2200 dollars. The 200 dollars will come out of the sale of my oxen.

Farming is too hazardous, too much of a gamble. Keeping cattle, young stock, is the only safe and certain way. I knew it and I was planning to go into ranching, right after receipt of the money. In an ordinary average year with an average rainfall I would have been able to do 1000 dollars' work with my horses and I would have made my expenses and my full wage. Now in this dry year I lost money and every dry year I will lose and become poor and in a good year I will make it all up again. Farming is too hazardous and ranching isn't. Naturally there are disadvantages to that too, but you hardly ever lose.

I'm talking now as a man who has worked things out. *There is enough money in farming with oxen, but there's no money if farming with horses.* In a good year a man may make some, but he is sure to lose it again in a bad year. If I had done as I would have done, and should have done, I would have made money this year. I would have had about as much land broken as I have now, if I had kept the oxen. Then I could have broken a lot of land in the wet weather, while now I had to sit. Besides that I would have made money with my cattle. Now that the States have been so friendly as to open their boundaries for Canadian cattle, we've acquired a big market and the prices are good. I would really like to sell my horses in early spring, fence my land, and go to Winnipeg for cattle, but the market for horses is poor and the prices have really gone down since this spring and summer. There's no money in the country, borrowing money is difficult, crops are poor this year, even though the papers say 'the very thing' is lovely.

HOME, 10 DECEMBER 1913

We've had beautiful weather here so far this December, and because
the ground is so dry and we still haven't had any snow, you can still
work on the land. I'm busy discing and harrowing again, and it's
really going quite well for the time of year. The winter is a long
enough period for me and the horses to sit still, so we're keeping
busy as long as we can. If the weather stay like it is, I'll keep working and discing.

This year's crop of oats taught me how desirable it is to have the
land in good condition in a dry year, before you sow your crop. If I
hadn't harrowed it as often as I did last fall, then I certainly
wouldn't have had such a good crop. It all depends on whether
you've gotten the ground fine and even, so the rain sinks into it
easily, and the land holds the moisture. If it's dry again next year,
then my land will still be in such a condition that I can expect a
fairly good crop.

The horses are holding up well and look very good. A little work
like that does them good, and after I've unharnessed them at night, I
let them run loose for an hour or so. And even after they've worked
a whole day they jump and dance and roll around with all four legs
in the air (it's a real pleasure to watch them). Still it's a risky enter-
prise to let all four loose at the same time; you have to watch the
mares.

If H. is coming, I'd advise him to travel second class, one always
gets through the immigration authorities much easier, and by Colon-
ist car on the train (cheapest). And don't let him take anything with
him that even at a distance looks like baggage. Really impress this
upon him. Let him wear a good suit of clothes and a good pair of
shoes, and let him put on clean underwear the day he leaves Holland.
And if it seems to have gotten a little dirty by the time he reaches
Canada, he can buy a clean outfit here; you can get it in a shop on
the boat.

There's a piano player in the Moving Picture show in Morse who
earns 60 dollars a month, for playing from 8 to 11 every evening,
and he's only a second-class pianist in a little town like Morse.

A Dutch Homesteader on the Prairies

Willem de Gelder

Translated and introduced
by Herman Ganzevoort

The letters in this volume, found in
the original Dutch in the archives of the
Netherlands Emigration Service in
Holland, form a unique chronicle of
the life of one European homesteader
in Saskatchewan from 1910 to 1913.
They were written by Willem de Gelder
whose experience as a homesteader
was typical of that of hundreds of
thousands of newcomers to the prairies
in the greatest years of western expansion just before the First World War.
As a European immigrant he was able
to write from a special perspective often
ignored in Anglo-Saxon accounts of
western development.

Minute and perceptive observations
of daily life are contained in his letters;
together with the recollections of
friends and neighbours who spoke well
of him, this volume forms the portrait
of a singular man who personified the
toughness and persistence of the
western pioneer.